New Da...

C000001338

Edited by **Gordon Giles** September–December 2023

BRF

15 The Chambers, Vineyard,
Abingdon OX14 3FE
brf.org.uk

Bible Reading Fellowship is a charity (233280)
and company limited by guarantee (301324),
registered in England and Wales

ISBN 978 1 80039 181 9
All rights reserved

Distributed in Australia by:
MediaCom Education Inc, PO Box 610, Unley, SA 5061
Tel: 1 800 811 311 | admin@mediacom.org.au

Distributed in New Zealand by:
Scripture Union Wholesale, PO Box 760, Wellington 6140
Tel: 04 385 0421 | suwholesale@clear.net.nz

Acknowledgements
Scripture quotations marked with the following abbreviations are taken from the
version shown. **NIV:** The Holy Bible, New International Version, Anglicised edition,
copyright © 1979, 1984, 2011 by Biblica. Used by permission of Hodder & Stoughton
Publishers, an Hachette UK company. All rights reserved. 'NIV' is a registered
trademark of Biblica. UK trademark number 1448790. **NRSV:** New Revised Standard
Version Updated Edition. Copyright © 2021 National Council of Churches of Christ
in the United States of America. Used by permission. All rights reserved.
ESV: The Holy Bible, English Standard Version, published by HarperCollins
Publishers, © 2001 Crossway Bibles, a division of Good News Publishers. Used by
permission. All rights reserved. **MSG:** *The Message*, copyright © 1993, 1994, 1995,
1996, 2000, 2001, 2002 by Eugene H. Peterson. Used by permission of NavPress. All
rights reserved. Represented by Tyndale House Publishers, Inc.

A catalogue record for this book is available from the British Library

Printed by Gutenberg Press, Tarxien, Malta

Suggestions for using *New Daylight*

Find a regular time and place, if possible, where you can read and pray undisturbed. Before you begin, take time to be still and perhaps use the BRF prayer on page 6. Then read the Bible passage slowly (try reading it aloud if you find it over-familiar), followed by the comment. You can also use *New Daylight* for group study and discussion, if you prefer.

The prayer or point for reflection can be a starting point for your own meditation and prayer. Many people like to keep a journal to record their thoughts about a Bible passage and items for prayer. In *New Daylight* we also note the Sundays and some special festivals from the church calendar, to keep in step with the Christian year.

New Daylight and the Bible

New Daylight contributors use a range of Bible versions, and you will find a list of the versions used opposite. You are welcome to use your own preferred version alongside the passage printed in the notes. This can be particularly helpful if the Bible text has been abridged.

New Daylight affirms that the whole of the Bible is God's revelation to us, and we should read, reflect on and learn from every part of both Old and New Testaments. Usually the printed comment presents a straightforward 'thought for the day', but sometimes it may also raise questions rather than simply providing answers, as we wrestle with some of the more difficult passages of scripture.

New Daylight is also available in a deluxe edition (larger format). Visit your local Christian bookshop or BRF's online shop **brfonline.org.uk**. To obtain a cassette version for the visually impaired, contact Torch Trust for the Blind, Torch House, Torch Way, Northampton Road, Market Harborough LE16 9HL; +44 (0)1858 438260; **info@torchtrust.org**. For a Braille edition, contact St John's Guild, Sovereign House, 12–14 Warwick Street, Coventry CV5 6ET; +44 (0)24 7671 4241; **info@stjohnsguild.org**.

Comment on *New Daylight*

To send feedback, please email **enquiries@brf.org.uk**, phone **+44 (0)1865 319700** or write to the address shown opposite.

Writers in this issue

Steve Aisthorpe is the Church of Scotland's mission development worker for the Highlands and Islands. He was previously executive director of the International Nepal Fellowship and is the author of *The Invisible Church* (St Andrew Press, 2016).

Amy Boucher Pye is an author, speaker and spiritual director. She's a regular contributor to several devotional publications and her books include *7 Ways to Pray*, *The Living Cross* and *Celebrating Christmas*.

Ruth Hassall is a speaker, trainer, author and coach with over 20 years' experience of working with individuals, churches, organisations and dioceses.

Margot Hodson is director of theology and education for The John Ray Initiative (JRI) and a vicar in Oxfordshire. She is on the boards of A Rocha UK and Grove Ethics Editorial Group.

Martin Hodson is a plant scientist and environmental biologist, and JRI's operations director. The Hodsons regularly speak on the environment to Christian audiences.

Bob Mayo is the Anglican prison chaplain at HMP Wormwood Scrubs.

Ross Moughtin served in the same parish in Liverpool for 26 years, where with his wife Jacqui he led 50 Alpha courses. With four daughters, they have nine granddaughters and just one grandson.

Roland Riem is vice-dean of Winchester Cathedral. He has oversight for education and green issues and has been much involved with colleagues in enabling the cathedral to recover from the Covid-19 pandemic.

Sheila Walker has been a teacher, editor, single parent, author, information officer, grandmother and is currently serving as associate minister with three rural churches. She enjoys words, walking and holidays in Wales.

Sally Welch is diocesan canon of Christ Church Cathedral, Oxford and co-director of the Centre for Christian Pilgrimage. She is the former editor of *New Daylight*.

Gordon Giles writes...

Each edition of *New Daylight* is prepared about a year in advance. So as I write this, we are in the midst of the national period of mourning for the late Queen Elizabeth II. You will likely be reading this as we approach the first anniversary – the 'year's mind'– of her passing. This will be keenly felt by many, not least by the king and his family.

Summarising Colin Murray Parkes, the late queen reminded us after the horrors of 9/11 that 'grief is the price we pay for love'. There was genuine grief at the death of Her Majesty, because there was genuine love. Wherever there is a level of love, there is a gradient of grief.

There is something fundamentally human about the marking of time and the keeping of anniversaries. We can only assume that no other creature does it, and it was only in the last few centuries that we humans became clock-time measured, driven even. Twice a year, in March and October, we put our clocks forward or back. It is a strange, but normal activity. It is seasonal, and it marks the division of the year, beyond our control yet which we accept, complying without complaint or resistance. It is comforting in October, as we gain a 'lie in', although there is chronological payback in March, when we have to get up earlier as the clocks go forward! We live by the clock and the calendar. Nevertheless we have always measured and marked the seasons.

Now we travel from autumn to Advent and move through the November 'kingdom season', when those who have died – naturally, tragically, in war or peace – are remembered nationally, locally and privately. And although the idea of a 'kingdom season' was invented by the church as recently as 1917, it is fitting that at this time of year, as leaves turn brown and fall, we are reminded of the kingdom of God and of Christ our King, in whose kingdom we already dwell and shall come to dwell. For then we can truly celebrate Christmas in a spirit of faith, hope and love.

Gordon

REVD CANON DR GORDON GILES

The BRF Prayer

Faithful God,
thank you for growing BRF
from small beginnings
into a worldwide family of ministries.
We rejoice as young and old
discover you through your word
and grow daily in faith and love.
Keep us humble in your service,
ambitious for your glory
and open to new opportunities.
For your name's sake,
Amen.

Helping to pay it forward

As part of our Living Faith ministry, we're raising funds to give away copies of Bible reading notes and other resources to those who aren't able to access them any other way, working with food banks and chaplaincy services, in prisons, hospitals and care homes.

If you've enjoyed and benefited from our resources, would you consider paying it forward to enable others to do so too?

Make a gift at **brf.org.uk/donate**

Autumn

 I will try not to wax too lyrical about autumn. Those seasonal mists can be chilling and persistent, and the mellow fruitfulness an avalanche of worm-eaten windfalls. If you live nearer the equator, it may not look that different from other seasons, and if you are further south again, well, our September may look more like your March.

Nevertheless, I have to admit that autumn in England is my favourite season: probably for reasons that do me little credit. The chief of these is a sense that the weight of expectation is somehow lifted. Spring would seem to invite new enterprise; summer is the season to bring it to pass, and there is always a subconscious fear of failure, in some unspecified way. But by autumn I can relax. The die is cast, or not; the seeds are sown, or not; they will flourish and fruit, or not. Whatever: there is nothing more to be done, except to await the harvest, with hope and equanimity.

It is also an intermediate season; usually, no extremes of heat or cold, dark or light. No need to concern myself with sun cream or sheepskin mitts. I can wear jeans and sweatshirts and take a more relaxed approach to life. More time, perhaps, to appreciate everyday wonders, and the particular ambience of autumn.

Whether or not this bears any relation to a spiritual autumn – which, given my stage of life, must now be upon me – is a matter of debate. The Bible does not elaborate on autumn in so many words, though patterns of day and night, sun and rain, times and seasons are regularly to be found, from the creation accounts in Genesis to the parables of Jesus in the gospels. It has nevertheless been an interesting exercise for me to explore some of the thoughts and feelings associated with autumn in the light of scripture. My hope is that the results may also prove fruitful in sparking your imagination and encouraging you to forage for and find spiritual food in unexpected places.

SHEILA WALKER

Colour wheel

For everything there is a season and a time for every matter under heaven: a time to be born and a time to die; a time to plant and a time to pluck up what is planted; a time to kill and a time to heal; a time to break down and a time to build up; a time to weep and a time to laugh; a time to mourn and a time to dance.

Autumn is late in middle England this year. I am writing in mid-November, and the leaves are only now beginning to take on those subtle, non-primary colours which call for the vocabulary of the artist's palette: burnt sienna, russet, amber, burnt umber, gold, vermilion. It is a selective palette; other colours are missing. I am reminded of my autumn wedding, when friends decked the church in these warm autumn colours. But on the wedding morning, a friend who was working abroad sent bright pink Singapore orchids; they were beautiful, but where to put them? Here, they were out of place; it was not the right season.

This leaves me with two thoughts. First, every season of our lives has its own particular colouring, as the writer of Ecclesiastes suggests. Those colours may or may not be to our liking, but it is important to learn to appreciate them, for each has its special place and qualities. True, a particular autumn may be golden, glowing and deeply gratifying, or it may be dun-coloured, damp and depressing. But just as the sun continues its work beyond the clouds, so God continues his work in every place and season. If only we may be given the grace to perceive it!

Looking back over your life, I wonder how you would paint or weave it; what colours would depict different times and seasons? To some extent, we choose our palette; some will have a penchant for darker or more subtle colours, others for bright ones, depending not only on our temperament but also on our willingness to trust that God is indeed a God of, and for, all seasons.

Lord, your creation reveals you as the supreme artist. Help me to trust the work of your Holy Spirit in colouring the seasons of my life.

SHEILA WALKER

Add seasoning

Happy are those who do not follow the advice of the wicked or take the path that sinners tread or sit in the seat of scoffers, but their delight is in the law of the Lord, and on his law they meditate day and night. They are like trees planted by streams of water, which yield their fruit in its season, and their leaves do not wither. In all that they do, they prosper.

The world is divided into those who enjoy spicy food and those who cannot stand it. Seasoning, one might argue, is a matter of taste and, as far as food is concerned, the privileged among us can choose. That does not apply to life in general, however, where we so often have little control over the seasons, and therefore seasoning, which we are asked to accept.

So how might we cope with those more unpalatable times and seasons? How might we succeed in yielding fruit in each season? The psalmist has a 'do' and a 'don't' for us to consider.

First, *don't* keep the wrong company. This does not mean shutting ourselves away from the rest of the world in some kind of Christian bunker, but it does mean not listening to ungodly words, not stepping out on the basis of misleading encouragements and not falling into or indulging a cynical mindset. That may mean no shortcuts, no easy escape from challenging circumstances, no pleasing the peer group: tough.

Second, *do* focus on the 'law of the Lord'. This speaks not merely of a nodding acquaintance with the ten commandments, but a continual mulling over whatever part of scripture the Lord may highlight. God's words, born out of his loving desire to reveal himself to us, are to become our delight, because they will lead us into life in all its fullness and fruitfulness.

Naturally speaking, we are bound to find certain seasons and seasonings of our lives more or less congenial. As I write, there is a gale blowing and sleet in the air – but the Lord can be in the wind or earthquake as much as in the still small voice (see 1 Kings 19:11–12).

Lord, may I be willing to receive whatever seasoning you may choose to add depth and piquancy to my life and witness.

SHEILA WALKER

Never too late

'For the kingdom of heaven is like a landowner who went out early in the morning to hire labourers for his vineyard. After agreeing with the labourers for a denarius for the day, he sent them into his vineyard… And about five o'clock he went out and found others standing around, and he said to them, "Why are you standing here idle all day?" They said to him, "Because no one has hired us." He said to them, "You also go into the vineyard."'

I love this parable, because the labourers who were not unwilling to work, but had simply lacked the opportunity, were not only welcomed at this late hour but also paid the same as everyone else. Truly, no one is overlooked or under-rewarded by God.

Going round the local garden centre, I feel strangely moved by those shrubs and plants labelled 'late flowering' – somehow full of admiration that they have not given up, have not been upstaged by those early bright young things. I am moved, even, to buy some! Maybe because I and many I know have experienced something of this 'late flowering' in our own lives. We are autumn, rather than spring or summer people.

The labourers did not choose to be idle; had they not been willing to work, they would not have been standing around in the marketplace, hopeful and available. And that is what God asks of us: hopefulness, which is based on trust, and availability. Just as our good shepherd leaves the 99 sheep and goes looking for the one (Luke 15:1–7), so he will also not forget the one who may appear to have been left behind by the crowd. They too will have their moment; and those years of waiting will, in his economy, so often turn out to have been part of the preparation.

The glorious truth is that, with God, it is never too late – never too late to turn around, never too late to launch out, never too late to love, cry, write a book, mend a friendship, respond to God's latest invitation. Our times are in God's hands, and there you are never too old and it is never too late.

Lord, may our choices reflect our hopes, not our fears.
(Adapted from the words of Nelson Mandela, 1918–2013).

SHEILA WALKER

Water aid

'If you will only heed his every commandment that I am commanding you today – loving the Lord your God and serving him with all your heart and with all your soul – then he will give the rain for your land in its season, the early rain and the later rain… Take care, or you will be seduced into turning away, serving other gods and worshipping them, for then the anger of the Lord will be kindled against you, and he will shut up the heavens, so that there will be no rain.'

Moses' words about the early and later rain, the spring and autumn rain, are echoed by Jeremiah and Joel: rain is a blessing from God, essential for life and fruitfulness – whatever we may feel when it blows in at inconvenient times or brings disaster in its wake.

In these passages we are told of an ordered pattern of seasonal weather, a degree of predictability which enables the farmer to prepare, to plan and plant and be sure of a good harvest. While not wishing to go into the debate about climate change in any detail, it is worth noting that this is certainly not what we are often experiencing now, even if certain parts of the world are shielded from the worst extremes of drought and flooding. Could this have anything to do with the worship of other gods – the gods of materialism or commercial interest?

In our own lives, too, we need rain, literally and spiritually: that is, the refreshing of God's Holy Spirit, the living water. Our honest desire is that we may be fruitful, may produce those fruits of the Spirit, may have a harvest to offer to God. But it can seem like a struggle. We have probably all known times when, like Gerard Manley Hopkins, our lives seem dry, disappointing, barren even. At those moments we echo his prayer: 'Mine, O thou Lord of life, send my roots rain.'

Creator God, may my roots be deep and firm; with joy may I draw water from your well of salvation, so that I may be thankful, fruitful and share your generous love with all those whose lives are touched by mine. Amen

SHEILA WALKER

Falling forwards

So we do not lose heart. Even though our outer nature is wasting away, our inner nature is being renewed day by day. For this slight, momentary affliction is producing for us for an eternal weight of glory beyond all measure, because we look not at what can be seen but at what cannot be seen, for what can be seen is temporary, but what cannot be seen is eternal. For we know that, if the earthly tent we live in is destroyed, we have a building from God, a house not made with hands, eternal in the heavens.

For some people autumn can be a somewhat depressing time – a time of wasting away, when the few remaining green leaves are crumpled by frost and it is not only the ash trees that are dying back. Fall, as the Americans call it, can be seen – and lamented – as the herald of winter, when so much is closed down, put into cold storage.

But this is far from being Paul's message to the Christians at Corinth. Not only will life have its seasonal ups and downs, but our life itself will have its autumn season, its physical wasting away as we approach our three score years and ten, if we are so blessed or, sadly, sometimes earlier. But this is not something to be lamented, for even these years of shedding, slowing, settling are, in God's economy, productive. Just as fallen leaves, oak and beech mast, and varying types of compost act as nutrients for both soil and animal life, so our dying back is enabling new, inner growth, if we will embrace it.

It may be true that we never really know how strong our faith is until it becomes a matter of life and death: and it can be inspirational to glimpse the radiance of faith in a dying saint. The fact of death as the gateway to true life is of course integral to Christianity, centred as it is on the cross. Dying is the only way to get there.

Lord of all life, may we see our dying, whatever form it may take, as so many steps towards the heavenly home which you have prepared for us, with its eternal weight of glory.

SHEILA WALKER

Crop circles

Do not be deceived; God is not mocked, for you reap whatever you sow. If you sow to your own flesh, you will reap corruption from the flesh, but if you sow to the Spirit, you will reap eternal life from the Spirit. So let us not grow weary in doing what is right, for we will reap at harvest time, if we do not give up. So then, whenever we have an opportunity, let us work for the good of all and especially for those of the family of faith.

In the church's year, autumn speaks of harvest and harvest festivals. One of our tiny village churches sees its congregation multiplied by five, with its harvest loaves made from wheat grown in the nearby fields. It is reminiscent of another era, perhaps, but a salutary reminder that we do indeed reap what we sow and that, in addition to all the farmers' hard work, we are dependent on God for the soil, sun and rain to enable those seeds to grow.

Few of us are actually farmers, with that intimate knowledge of the natural world and our need to cooperate with it and our dependence upon it, but the metaphor of sowing and reaping holds good, whatever our work or circumstances. 'Sowing' relates to all our choices, whether in thought, word or deed and whether heartfelt or hopeful as we seek to challenge and change our reluctant hearts and self-interest. You may well know the saying by Ralph Waldo Emerson: 'Sow a thought, reap an action; sow an action, reap a habit; sow a habit, reap a character; sow a character, reap a destiny.' One thing leads to another, often imperceptibly.

Experience tells us that virtue is not always rewarded immediately. However diligent our sowing, we do not necessarily see all the harvest which will eventually result from it: that will be known only when we enter fully into that eternal life which is the gift of the Spirit. Not to persevere, though, is to compromise our own integrity and undermine the work of the Spirit in restoring the image of Christ in us.

Creator God, grant us the grace, discernment and courage to sow seeds of faith, hope and love wherever and whenever we have the opportunity, trusting you for the harvest.

SHEILA WALKER

A ripe old age?

God chose to make known how great among the gentiles are the riches of the glory of this mystery, which is Christ in you, the hope of glory. It is he whom we proclaim, warning everyone and teaching everyone in all wisdom, so that we may present everyone mature in Christ. For this I toil and strive with all the energy that he powerfully inspires within me.

Autumn sees many crops reaching maturity; yes, it is often possible nowadays to force an earlier harvest, but it is rarely as good as the one that ripens naturally. It may mean a bit of competition with the wasps to get there first, but it is worth it.

To be presented 'mature in Christ' is a good way of expressing our calling as Christians. To be sure, it is true that in Christ we are in one sense already new creations, but we do not arrive ready-made, complete in every detail. We are more like a fresh lump of clay, to be moulded, shaped, fired, glazed; a work in progress. In the autumn of our lives, we will find ourselves being shaped in ways that were not possible before the onset of age and experience. The season may take many different forms depending on our work, family and health, but every situation will contain within it the potential for growing in Christlike maturity, if we can only welcome and accept those opportunities.

I can remember at primary school being given as a prize a book called *Growing Up Gracefully*. I was not impressed! I recognise now, though, that it can be quite a challenge to grow old gracefully. Are grey hairs to be disguised or welcomed? Is it for better or worse that I am slowing down? One of the greatest gains is surely a reassessment of perspective, of what really matters most: character above achievement; wisdom above knowledge; the ripeness of the fruit of the Spirit in my life; a greater awareness of what constitutes true Christian maturity.

Lord Jesus Christ, may I have the grace to welcome every situation as an opportunity to grow and mature into all that you intend for me, so that others may catch a glimpse of your glory.

SHEILA WALKER

Apple pie

I call upon you, for you will answer me, O God; incline your ear to me; hear my words. Wondrously show your steadfast love, O saviour of those who seek refuge from their adversaries at your right hand. Guard me as the apple of the eye; hide me in the shadow of your wings, from the wicked who despoil me, my deadly enemies who surround me.

Originally the 'apple of the eye' referred simply to the pupil, and this is true of the majority of references in the Bible. The apple reference seems to have originated from English, possibly around the ninth century. In either case, though, the meaning is something or someone that is cherished above all else.

Certainly apples are more characteristic of the UK than Israel or Palestine; what could be more British than apple pie? My children used to bewail the fact that, come autumn, apples seem to find their way into every meal in one form or another. But there is surely something truly refreshing, heartening, humbling even about being able to enjoy simple food that is often there for the picking, a gift from God (perhaps via a kind neighbour). We have grown accustomed to being able to enjoy such a variety of food from all over the world – spicy, exotic, in and out of season – but there is perhaps a need to recover our appreciation of what is simple, good and on our doorstep.

The way in which different cultures and countries translate this phrase may vary according to what is most valued, most enjoyed, most precious: whatever best reflects the delight and value that God experiences and places on his people. Here, I see no reason to look further than the apple (no, it was not actually an apple that was Eve's undoing). With over 7,500 different varieties to reflect our diversity, we are well served. Maybe you can find a perfect apple and take a moment simply to look and wonder, as did the old masters who created such wonderful still life paintings. Also reflect on the fact that it is with just such wonder, care and delight that God looks on you.

Creator God, remind me in this apple season of the simple goodness of your love for us: unconditional, nourishing and generous. Grace indeed. May we eat and be forever thankful.

SHEILA WALKER

Preserves

I treasure your word in my heart, so that I may not sin against you. Blessed are you, O Lord; teach me your statutes. With my lips I declare all the ordinances of your mouth. I delight in the way of your decrees as much as in all riches. I will meditate on your precepts and fix my eyes on your ways. I will delight in your statutes; I will not forget your word.

Autumn is the season for storing up, for filling the shelves against the deprivations of winter, for bottling and preserving those apples, plums, damsons, berries and so much more: jam, cordial, chutney, marmalade, gin… for ourselves, the fete, Christmas presents. Now there is abundance, but there could be lean times ahead, so it makes sense to lay up some stores. It can be hard work – all those currants to de-stalk, tomatoes to skin, and maybe to search the recipe books for ways of using more unusual things like medlars or quince.

David has the same approach to the word of God: not only to read it but to treasure it, meditate on it, store it up in his heart so that it is there to be drawn upon in any time of need. For us, too, it is important not simply to read, but to mark, learn and inwardly digest scripture. And perhaps it is good, too, not always to go back to our favourite passages in Psalms or the gospels but to explore some of those less frequented parts of our Bibles, which can also produce sustaining fare.

What is in your spiritual store-cupboard? A friend who was (wrongly) imprisoned drew heavily on his memory of liturgy and hymns to sustain himself; and I am always shamed by those Christians with very limited access to a Bible who have learned whole gospels by heart. It is surely worth the autumn work of storing up in order to have a word in season for all seasons.

Lord, our provider, thank you for all the nourishment contained in the scriptures. Help us to draw from them all that we need in order to serve you and one another, all year round, with energy, wisdom and grace.

SHEILA WALKER

John the Baptist

 Allow me to introduce my friend John. Well, I say 'friend', but he is not always thought of as anyone's friend, nor even as being particularly friendly. John is one of those awkward people about whom you are never quite sure: outspoken, unpredictable, idiosyncratic, 'different'. His life and manners tally as the outcome of a unique heritage, upbringing and calling. Born to aged parents, he would have been brought up carefully and strictly, inheriting both his father's piety and questioning of authority. Led into the wilderness, most likely in Qumran's rocky desert, he ate the only food there was, and, away from the hustle and bustle of contemporary Jewish life and worship, he cut a solitary figure, calling for repentance and amendment of life.

Sometimes called 'the captain of prophets', he stands at the head of the line of prophetic speech and action which points to and culminates in Christ. Like Elijah, Jeremiah and Isaiah before him, he said and did things which others disliked. Ultimately it cost him his life, not because he heralded Jesus, but because he challenged the immoral behaviour of King Herod. Because he spoke moral authority to regal power and paid the price, he is thought of as a kind of martyr, suffering for the right. Thus he is a model and precursor of all those who, as Jesus was to put it, 'are persecuted for the sake of righteousness' (Matthew 5:10, NRSV). Although revered as a saint, he was not a disciple of Jesus and did not live long enough to see and testify to the risen Christ (but nor did St Joseph for that matter). Yet his role and contribution to the story of salvation is immense and vital.

Here then is John. You might not 'like' him, but you have to admire him. You might not like the questions he asks, the challenges he raises, his dress sense or the bluntness of his tone. The manner of his death is horrible and unnecessary. This makes him a man for our times too. John is unique, but also representative of so many good and devoted people who have loved peace and truth, breathed God's Spirit, testified to Christ, but ultimately had their earthly light evilly snuffed out by the darkly powerful. Yet we rejoice with him in the greater light of his friend Jesus Christ in whom he hoped and heralded.

GORDON GILES

Conception

'Zechariah… your prayer has been heard, and your wife Elizabeth will bear you a son, and you shall call his name John. And you will have joy and gladness, and many will rejoice at his birth, for he will be great before the Lord. And he must not drink wine or strong drink, and he will be filled with the Holy Spirit, even from his mother's womb. And he will turn many of the children of Israel to the Lord their God, and he will go before him in the spirit and power of Elijah, to turn the hearts of the fathers to the children, and the disobedient to the wisdom of the just, to make ready for the Lord a people prepared.'

As is the case with several of the prophets, John's story begins before his birth. It points backwards and forwards. Backwards to Jeremiah, of whom we read 'Before I formed you in the womb I knew you' (Jeremiah 1:5), and forwards a mere six months to Mary's annunciation. John appears at a testamental crossroads, and his emergence is pivotal, as he looks in both directions. Although special and prophetic, these words also speak of something ordinary and definitive. We are all known in the womb by God, whose love for us and calling into life is simultaneously individual and universal. Like John, our arrival is known by parents before we conceive of our own being, but we herald the beginnings of our own existence with internal stirrings in the womb.

For John, there is detail: there is to be no alcoholic spirit for him, but rather the Holy Spirit of God. This first New Testament reference to the Spirit prefigures John's role as the baptiser of Jesus at which the Spirit descends. This reference to the Spirit before John is born presages a cumulative handover. For the Spirit will not leave John, but in his presence at Jesus' baptism the Spirit will descend on him too. Jesus will be baptised by John, adopt his practice and relate to him until the end of his life. It is almost as if, briefly, there will be a handover period, overseen by God's Spirit.

God, you have known us all our lives, even when we have not known ourselves. Send your Spirit to guide and help us all our days. Amen

GORDON GILES

Mary visits Elizabeth

In those days Mary arose and went with haste into the hill country, to a town in Judah, and she entered the house of Zechariah and greeted Elizabeth. And when Elizabeth heard the greeting of Mary, the baby leaped in her womb. And Elizabeth was filled with the Holy Spirit, and she exclaimed with a loud cry, 'Blessed are you among women, and blessed is the fruit of your womb! And why is this granted to me that the mother of my Lord should come to me? For behold, when the sound of your greeting came to my ears, the baby in my womb leaped for joy.'

One of the most famous pieces of music by Bach is 'Jesu, joy of man's desiring'. It comes from his 147th cantata, *Herz und Mund und Tat und Leben*, first performed in Leipzig on the Feast of the Visitation of the Blessed Virgin Mary, 2 July 1723. It commemorates this visit of Mary to her relative Elizabeth, pregnant with John the Baptist. The theme of the cantata is that 'heart and mouth and deed and life must bear witness to Christ without fear and hypocrisy that he is God and saviour'. There are two parts, both of which contain several sections of music, both of which culminate in a rendition of the chorale we know as 'Jesu, joy', played or sung at weddings and funerals today.

In Part Two is an aria in which John the Baptist is introduced as the one who, still inside his mother, recognises Jesus in Mary's womb and kicks accordingly. He cannot witness to Jesus other than by kicking, and Bach even depicts this kicking musically with the oboe! John cannot speak yet, but he stirs and leaps inside. The whole cantata is about not denying Christ and praising him in whatever way we can – even with our feet! None of us will ever do what John did inside Elizabeth, now, but it is likely that we all did before we were born, and perhaps we may say that even then we were exercising the first inner stirrings of faith in God, who has known and loved us even before we were born.

'It is good for me that I have Jesus: O how fast I hold to him'
('Jesu, joy of man's desiring' by J.S. Bach, 1685–1750).

GORDON GILES

Prophecy

'And you, child, will be called the prophet of the Most High; for you will go before the Lord to prepare his ways, to give knowledge of salvation to his people in the forgiveness of their sins, because of the tender mercy of our God, whereby the sunrise shall visit us from on high to give light to those who sit in darkness and in the shadow of death, to guide our feet into the way of peace.' And the child grew and became strong in spirit, and he was in the wilderness until the day of his public appearance to Israel.

To anyone brought up in the Anglican tradition of the *Book of Common Prayer*, these words will be deeply familiar. In cathedrals and parish churches they are said by those at Morning Prayer every day. Read from dusty prayer books, from modern editions or from the Daily Prayer app, these words circumnavigate the globe constantly. As the hymnwriter John Ellerton (1826–93) put it: 'As o'er each continent and island the dawn leads on another day, the voice of prayer is never silent, nor dies the strain of praise away.' For it is always morning somewhere on earth and there is always a group of people saying their prayers together at any time: 'The sun that bids us rest is waking our brethren 'neath the western sky, and hour by hour fresh lips are making thy wondrous doings heard on high.'

These are indeed wondrous doings which we speak or sing daily, the doings of God, who has muted and then opened the mouth of Zechariah. Like Thomas after him, he doubted and then, when presented with incontrovertible evidence, he praises God. 'Doubting' Thomas believes and says: 'My Lord and my God!' (John 20:28); 'believing' Zechariah sings this hymn.

Hymns are not always sung *to* God, nor are they always *about* God. This praise is addressed to baby John; it is a hymn because it extols the works of God, yet to be revealed, which also makes it prophetic. It is prophecy *about* a prophet, *to* a prophet, and Zechariah is the incredulous father who ought to be both proud and ashamed: proud of his son, and ashamed of his doubt.

Every day, Lord, may we praise you, ashamed of our sins,
but proud of the knowledge of salvation you have prepared for us. Amen

GORDON GILES

Preparing the way

'Behold, I send my messenger before your face, who will prepare your way, the voice of one crying in the wilderness: "Prepare the way of the Lord, make his paths straight."' John appeared, baptising in the wilderness and proclaiming a baptism of repentance for the forgiveness of sins. And all the country of Judea and all Jerusalem were going out to him and were being baptised by him in the river Jordan, confessing their sins. Now John was clothed with camel's hair and wore a leather belt around his waist and ate locusts and wild honey.

Nowadays we might be tempted to say that John was weird. Dishevelled, strangely dressed and living on an unusual diet, his being 'different' might make us cross the road or avoid his gaze. On the other hand, in recent years we have come to be more tolerant of difference and more generous-spirited towards those of whom we might be inclined to be apprehensive.

It is hard not to judge people by their appearance, and that Mark tells us what John wore and ate suggests that he would have cut a noticeably distinctive figure in his day: his contemporaries noticed his garb too. John was a common name, meaning 'graced by God', so this John is the John who dressed oddly. Did he not care about his appearance, or did he do it to get noticed? He also said uncomfortable things. Yet he was popular, people flocked to him because they warmed to his message and recognised their need of salvation. In spite of the unusual manner of his appearance and lifestyle, he was clearly blessed by God with a message that was authentic, powerful, necessary and welcome.

I'm reminded of the young Greta Thunberg, whom some people try to dismiss because of her youth and appearance, yet who has an uncomfortable, uncompromising message that is far more significant. Like John, she preaches a 'turning around' in attitude and behaviour concerning climate change. Many people flock to hear her and welcome her candid words advocating the need for personal and societal change.

God, help us to not judge others by what they look like, eat or wear, but rather let us recognise your face and hear your call of love in all whom we meet today. Amen

GORDON GILES

Jesus' best man

John answered, 'A person cannot receive even one thing unless it is given him from heaven. You yourselves bear me witness, that I said, "I am not the Christ, but I have been sent before him." The one who has the bride is the bridegroom. The friend of the bridegroom, who stands and hears him, rejoices greatly at the bridegroom's voice. Therefore this joy of mine is now complete. He must increase, but I must decrease.'

One of the most joyous days of my life was when I was the best man at the wedding of a dear friend, a fellow priest. My daughter (his godchild) was a bridesmaid. I was also asked to preach, so I had the rare and delightful privilege of giving both the sermon and the best man's speech!

The metaphor John uses hasn't changed. It is still conventional for the best man and the groom to give speeches. The groom has to thank everyone, and the best man is expected to tell stories and read out the telegrams and messages from absent friends. Traditionally the father of the bride speaks too, although nowadays the conventions are flexible: some brides or mothers or bride's best friend speak as well or instead, although it is rare for the groom or the best man not to do so. They are not competing: their roles and duties are different. The best man is expected to be funny, and the groom honest and complimentary. The best man rejoices when the groom speaks, because there is no greater honour than to be the best man. The best man (or chief bridesmaid) have things to do, but what they *do* is less important than who they *are*. It is all about being, rather than doing.

When Jesus met John at the Jordan there was a sense of handover, of ministry and mission, but it was not like a baton in a relay race whereby one lets go as another grasps. Rather it was a gradual process. Jesus increases and John decreases henceforward, but it is a joy, because he has not only *done* what he needed to do, he has *been*, and will continue to be, what he was called to be: the friend and forerunner.

May we, like John, also give way to Jesus. Amen

GORDON GILES

What you see is what you get

Now when John heard in prison about the deeds of the Christ, he sent word by his disciples and said to him, 'Are you the one who is to come, or shall we look for another?' And Jesus answered them, 'Go and tell John what you hear and see: the blind receive their sight and the lame walk, lepers are cleansed and the deaf hear, and the dead are raised up, and the poor have good news preached to them… What did you go out into the wilderness to see? A reed shaken by the wind?… A man dressed in soft clothing?… A prophet? Yes, I tell you, and more than a prophet.'

Now imprisoned by Herod, it seems that the bars of John's cage have rattled him, and he needs confirmation that all he has been doing, all he has stood for, is real and reliable. It would be no surprise if, imprisoned for the courage of his convictions, he questioned Jesus' authenticity. In his dingy, dark and doubtful place, he needs to know.

Jesus responds with clarity and compassion. His answer is in biblical code, referencing the messianic prophecies of Isaiah. 'Look,' he says. 'What I am is evidenced by what you see.' So the question about who Jesus *is* ('Are you the one?') is answered in terms of what he *does* (heal the sick, preach good news and so on).

Then, as Jesus often did, he turns the question around, asking his disciples: 'What did you expect to see? A nice man? Someone with no scruples who caves in under pressure?' Thus John's question becomes the catalyst for enabling Jesus to testify about him, to return the favour, as it were. The evidence that Jesus is the Christ is found in the healing and seeing and preaching. The evidence for John being the prophetic forerunner is his integrity, his conviction and his appearance. What you see is what you get, and what you get is what you see. Jesus tells them, and all posterity, that John is no fickle wanderer, but a man of supreme integrity, greater than the prophets before him. What an accolade from the Saviour of the world!

May we, like John, have our questions answered
in words and deeds. Amen

GORDON GILES

The end and beyond

Herod had seized John and bound him and put him in prison for the sake of Herodias, his brother Philip's wife, because John had been saying to him, 'It is not lawful for you to have her.' And though he wanted to put him to death, he feared the people, because they held him to be a prophet. But when Herod's birthday came, the daughter of Herodias danced before the company and pleased Herod, so that he promised with an oath to give her whatever she might ask... He sent and had John beheaded in the prison, and his head was brought on a platter and given to the girl, and she brought it to her mother.

This is the end of the line for John. It is a line that stretches back to the earliest prophets who spoke of the Messiah. It is poignant that the line of prophets, captained by John, should end abruptly as a direct and unequivocal consequence of that which necessitated the coming of the Messiah to whom they all witnessed: sin.

There is no mistaking it, no escaping it: John was someone who criticised a weak and cowardly king, who having committed the sin of adultery, succumbs to lust and so proceeds through pride to murder. It is horrific. Yet these things happen today. It is said that there were more Christian martyrs in the 20th century than in all the previous ones put together. John's brutal fate is archetypal: an anti-sacrament, the outward manifestation of an inner sin that can strike at any time.

However we cannot and must not leave John dead on a plate. Rather we remember – we re-member – him as the forerunner and friend who is midwife to the great sacrament of baptism – the simple, watery outworking of the inner grace given by God to each and every one of us who has received the life-giving Holy Spirit to serve and save us in this life and beyond.

God, in thanking you for the life and witness of John,
help us to join with Jesus in affirming his message,
accepting the call to repent of sins and receiving the gift
of the Holy Spirit to lead and inspire us into all life. Amen

GORDON GILES

Bible meals

 I was far older than I am happy to admit when I realised that the opening words to Handel's *Messiah* were in fact 'Comfort ye, comfort ye, my people', and not, as I had thought, 'Come for tea, come for tea, my people.' However, as I reflect on this, I am not sure that I was too far off the mark! Throughout the whole story of the Bible we read of the hospitality of God – the one who feeds weary prophets, sets tables before tired shepherds and ultimately invites anyone who would come to the greatest banquet imaginable.

As the Old Testament unfolds, and more of God's nature is made known, we find that hospitality is a key attribute of the character of God. And it is not hospitality in the way that we have maybe now come to understand it or imagine it to be – dinner parties with friends, where our Sunday best is put on show – but a hospitality that is essentially about inviting people into a covenant relationship with God's very self.

The hospitality of God is also a clear command that runs through the Old Testament. The people of God are to be those who extend a deep welcome to the foreigner living in the land. They are to be people who always look out for those that are not yet around the table, and to invite them in to take their place and to enjoy a good meal.

Over the next fortnight we shall be looking at some of these meals that demonstrate the multifaceted nature of the hospitality of God. We begin with some that are found in the Old Testament and we shall see how hospitality continues as a theme through Jesus' life. In the gospel of Luke, Jesus is never far from a meal, so that is where much of our focus will be.

I love the famous icon painted by Andrei Rublev that depicts the three persons of the Trinity seated around a table... with a spare place. As we spend time looking at some of the meals of the Bible, may we hear God's invitation to come, eat and enjoy, and then in turn be those who, by our lives, declare: 'There is always room for one more, you are so welcome here.'

RUTH HASSALL

Entertaining angels

Abraham looked up and saw three men standing nearby. When he saw them, he hurried from the entrance of his tent to meet them and bowed low to the ground. He said, 'If I have found favour in your eyes, my lord, do not pass your servant by. Let a little water be brought, and then you may all wash your feet and rest under this tree. Let me get you something to eat, so you can be refreshed and then go on your way – now that you have come to your servant.' 'Very well,' they answered, 'do as you say.'

According to the custom of the day, Abraham offers hospitality to three men who seemingly turn up randomly at his tent. As a good host, he offers water to wash his guests' feet, somewhere to rest in the shade and a good meal.

As the meal is prepared a conversation ensues, and as it unfolds Abraham realises that these are no ordinary visitors. Somehow they know Sarah's new name, that she is no longer called Sarai. They prophesy that Sarah will bear a son in the next year, although she is far too old for childbearing. This had been promised by the Lord to Sarah long before their visit, but how did they know?

As Abraham realises that he is not speaking to three ordinary visitors, the language in the story changes. At the beginning Abraham calls the men 'my lord' or 'sir', but then the story reveals it is the Lord, Yahweh, who is speaking.

When Abraham offers hospitality, he offers a delicious meal of freshly baked bread, the choicest meat and curds and milk. He ensures a comfortable place to sit and water to refresh and clean up. He does not realise he is welcoming the Lord to his meal. A good thing he did not simply get out a crust of stale bread and some grotty cheese! It is in the context of offering this hospitality that Abraham and Sarah receive an affirmation of the promise God had made to them.

May we be those who are quick to offer hospitality
(whatever that might look like), sharing our best as if with the Lord,
in gladness; and who knows who we might find around our table!

RUTH HASSALL

A stranger at the table

Ruth the Moabite said to Naomi, 'Let me go to the fields and pick up the leftover grain behind anyone in whose eyes I find favour'… So she went out, entered a field and began to glean behind the harvesters. As it turned out, she was working in a field belonging to Boaz, who was from the clan of Elimelek… At mealtime Boaz said to her, 'Come over here. Have some bread and dip it in the wine vinegar.' When she sat down with the harvesters, he offered her some roasted grain. She ate all she wanted and had some left over.

Ruth was a migrant living in a foreign land. She had travelled to Judah from Moab with her mother-in-law after the death of both their husbands. The two women were in terrible financial straits, struggling to survive. Ruth, determined to do something about their situation, went to the field to see if she could glean the corn. Without knowing it, the field that she chose 'just so happened' to belong to a relative of Naomi, Boaz. Boaz had heard about Ruth's loyalty to her mother-in-law and how she had left her homeland and come to live with a people she did not know before. He made sure she was safe from the men harvesting the field and that she had water to drink. At the meal time, Boaz offered her bread, wine vinegar to dip it in and roasted grain.

When Ruth went home and told Naomi about her day, Naomi said, 'The Lord bless him! He has not stopped showing his kindness to the living and the dead… He is one of our guardian-redeemers!' (v. 20). Boaz had gone above and beyond his duty.

In God's kingdom, there is always room at the table. Jesus was concerned for outsiders, the dispossessed, the poor. Who in your community might be afraid, left out, bereaved or without enough money to survive? How can we, as Boaz did, gently include and offer provision?

If you feel frightened, unable to be part of things, if you are mourning or if you are in want, Ruth's story gives us a firm hope that God's table has plenty of room for you.

RUTH HASSALL

The stuff of life

Elijah was afraid and ran for his life… He came to a broom brush, sat down under it and prayed that he might die. 'I have had enough, Lord,' he said… Then he lay down under the bush and fell asleep. All at once an angel touched him and said, 'Get up and eat.' He looked around, and there by his head was some bread baked over hot coals, and a jar of water. He ate and drank and then lay down again. Then the angel of the Lord came back a second time and touched him and said, 'Get up and eat, for the journey is too much for you'… Strengthened by that food, he travelled for forty days and forty nights until he reached Horeb, the mountain of God.

Elijah was exhausted, drained and in fear for his life. He had just been used by God in a spectacular way, and yet now he lay under a bush, asking God to let him die. God responded not by explaining why Elijah was wrong, point-ing out his faulty doctrine or delivering a detailed sermon, but simply by letting him rest and giving him food and drink. The balm for Elijah's weary soul was bread, the stuff of life, sustenance to nourish him. God did not tell him to get a grip, or to just get on with the job. He gave him good food, refreshing water and rest.

When people bring their big questions to God, when they air their despair and their fears, God so often invites them to come and eat and be sustained.

After Jesus' resurrection, when he met with Peter at a breakfast bar-beque on the beach (more on this next week), Jesus told him to, 'Feed my lambs… take care of my sheep… feed my sheep' (John 21:15–17). Providing nourishment, both physical and spiritual, is what God does for his people and calls us to do too.

If you are feeling like Elijah today, perhaps you could ask God to nourish you, body and soul. If you know someone who might feel like Elijah, perhaps you could invite them for a meal or a coffee and cake, and offer that space to be renewed and refreshed.

RUTH HASSALL

Glorious leftovers

A man came from Baal Shalishah, bringing the man of God twenty loaves of barley bread… 'Give it to the people to eat,' Elisha said. 'How can I set this before a hundred men?' his servant asked. But Elisha answered, 'Give it to the people to eat. For this is what the Lord says: "They will eat and have some left over."' Then he set it before them, and they ate and had some left over, according to the word of the Lord.

Elisha the prophet had returned to the famine-torn region of Gilgal. During times of hardship, sometimes terrible deeds are done. But often it is during the most difficult of times that generous gifts are beautifully shared: gifts which cost the giver greatly.

A man from Baal Shalishah brought Elisha 20 loaves of barley bread, baked from the first gatherings of the ripe corn harvest. What he could have kept for himself he brought as an offering. Elisha told the man to give the bread to the people to eat. But how could 20 loaves (and probably quite small ones at that) feed the people gathered there – a crowd of 100? This didn't faze Elisha. He told them to serve the bread, and to get ready because there would be leftovers to collect. And he was right. The bread was shared, the people got fed, and there was more than enough to go around.

As you read this passage, you may well hear echoes in your mind's ear of another story of a large crowd being fed. Fast forward to the New Testament and Jesus finds himself on a hill with 5,000 hungry men (not to mention women and children) needing some lunch. Once more the provision seems ridiculously inadequate, this time a mere five loaves and a couple of fish – yet, after that meal twelve baskets of leftovers are scooped up. One of the reasons this astounded the people was because it reminded them of the great prophet Elisha.

God can do amazing things with the gifts we give.
Can we have the same heart as the man from Baal Shalishah
and offer what is important and precious to us,
and trust that God will do with it more than we could imagine?

RUTH HASSALL

A day to feast

Then Nehemiah the governor, Ezra the priest and teacher of the Law, and the Levites who were instructing the people said to them all, 'This day is holy to the Lord your God. Do not mourn or weep.' For all the people had been weeping as they listened to the words of the Law. Nehemiah said, 'Go and enjoy choice food and sweet drinks, and send some to those who have nothing prepared. This day is holy to our Lord. Do not grieve, for the joy of the Lord is your strength.'

Celebration is a serious business. Nehemiah had been heartbroken when he received the news that Jerusalem was in ruins. He was heartbroken for the city, but even more so for the fear of the ruined reputation of God. He immediately set to work, enlisting the remnant left in Jerusalem to rebuild the walls and re-establish the city. In chapter 8, the work had been completed and the people all came together and asked Ezra the priest to read from the Book of the Law as they gathered. When they heard the reading they started to weep, as they realised just how long they had lived without the law of God while they were in exile.

Interestingly, Nehemiah does not affirm them in their mourning for the way in which things have been, but instead commands them to stop weeping and to start rejoicing. This was a day that was holy to the Lord, a day to feast and not to fast. Nehemiah knew that the people were now actively recommitting to following God, so they could put aside their sadness of heart and rejoice in thankfulness to God for his protection and provision. They were to celebrate God, give thanks for his goodness and share what they had with those who didn't have anything prepared.

For Nehemiah, celebration is an act of defiance in the face of the enemy that would seek to tear down and ruin. And today we can continue in that celebration. We can know that despite the outer circumstances God's joy can still be known and is our strength. It is a declaration of our confidence that God is near, and he is able to protect and provide.

---

*Lord, I pray that today, amid all that is going on, you would quieten
my heart and help me to know your joy as my strength.
Thank you for your closeness and your faithfulness. Amen.*

RUTH HASSALL

A table prepared

You prepare a table before me in the presence of my enemies. You anoint my head with oil; my cup overflows. Surely your goodness and love will follow me all the days of my life, and I will dwell in the house of the Lord forever.

Psalm 23 is a psalm of David. It was written out of his experience of being a boy shepherd, alone on the hills with the responsibility of looking after a flock of sheep. Those were desperate, dark times in which to live. As we read through the story of David we find that he was a man familiar with the reality of being pursued by enemies, whether they were his brothers, an angry giant, a jealous king or enemies on the battlefield. He knew what it was to face peril and harm. Here in this passage we see God preparing a meal, a feast, for the weary shepherd to sit and eat and rejoice. The provisions are generous, not measly. The cup overflows. God is good and generous, even when the enemy are round about.

The psalm is not asking us to turn a blind eye to dark valleys and evil situations. It is not asking us to make light of grief and loss. It is not trying to put a glib, Pollyanna spin on everything. But it is a deep, grateful, humble declaration recognising that God is with us and that he still prepares a table to sustain us and bring joy to our hearts, even in the hardest of situations.

These are some of the most famous words in the world. Psalm 23 has been used in times of celebration and at funerals. The text does not speak of an anonymous force for good, but a living, personal God, who rejoices in walking beside those in difficulty and darkness, preparing a meal and demonstrating his overflowing goodness and love.

The provision of a meal in difficult times continues to be a practical way in which care and love are shown to those in our communities, and can often speak louder than words of consolation to those that are struggling.

How have you known God's provision during difficult times?
Is there anyone today to whom you can demonstrate God's love in this practical way?

RUTH HASSALL

An open invitation

'Come, all you who are thirsty, come to the waters; and you who have no money, come, buy and eat! Come, buy wine and milk without money and without cost. Why spend money on what is not bread, and your labour on what does not satisfy? Listen, listen to me, and eat what is good, and you will delight in the richest of fare. Give ear and come to me; listen, that you may live. I will make an everlasting covenant with you, my faithful love promised to David.'

What a ridiculously, astonishingly generous offer, beautifully available to all! The only thing you need to do is to accept. God is offering refreshment and nourishment to anyone who would receive it. For what God is offering cannot be bought. Power, money and position are useless to help you access this glorious meal, the richest of fare. The people that will be given this will not be the strong, the self-sufficient, those seeking what will not satisfy, but the thirsty, the broken, those who are willing to come to God and recognise their need.

Isaiah is recording what he sees God saying to the people of Israel who, time and again, drifted away from depending on and obeying God as they sought to be self-sufficient and to manage their affairs without reference to God. God responds with this generous offer as part of his covenant with the people. But they need to accept it to receive it.

Sometimes the offers we hear advertised seem too good to be true, and largely that is because they are! Hidden within them is some catch, some clause that sees you inadvertently signing up for something buried in the small print. It is not so with the offer that God makes. The invitation is for us to see through the false offers made by the consumer culture of our day, which always promises more than it can deliver and never brings the satisfaction we so desperately crave, and to receive his truly satisfying fare.

Many people spend huge amounts of energy and money pursuing a lifestyle that they believe will be lifegiving, but which they are then too exhausted or financially stretched to enjoy.

Are you thirsty for life-giving water? God's offer of refreshment
and nourishment remains. Come, eat and enjoy!

RUTH HASSALL

A meal of celebration

Jesus went out and saw a tax collector by the name of Levi sitting at his tax booth. 'Follow me,' Jesus said to him, and Levi got up, left everything and followed him. Then Levi held a great banquet for Jesus at his house, and a large crowd of tax collectors and others were eating with them. But the Pharisees and the teachers of the law… complained to his disciples, 'Why do you eat and drink with tax collectors and sinners?'

As we read through the gospels we are left in little doubt that Jesus enjoyed social gatherings. So when Levi hosts a great banquet in his honour, we are not surprised that Jesus attends. However, the religious people of the day were not so pleased with Jesus' apparent lack of discretion about whose hospitality he was willing to receive, and the company he was content to keep.

It is fair to say that tax collectors were not known to be the most honest of folk and were often mentioned in the same breath as murderers and robbers, but that did not seem to trouble Jesus. Meeting Jesus had changed Levi's life and transformed his priorities and values. His instinctive response was to invite his friends, fellow tax collectors, to come and meet this man whose life and message was so compelling that Levi would leave his life behind with a backward glance. It was a day of celebration, a moment that had to be marked. A banquet needed to be thrown.

The real tragedy of this story is that those who were trying their hardest to be holy, to be acceptable before God and strict observers of the law were the ones who missed out on the grace of God, unable to rejoice with those who had been radically transformed by their encounter with Jesus.

These passages often present me with a huge challenge, and I find myself reflecting on Bishop Tom Wright's invitation not only to read the gospels for the stories that they are, but to read them again, hearing Jesus ask the question, 'How are we doing on this?' Who are the Levis in my life? Do I sometimes miss the grace of God when I try to earn his love, rather than live in response to it?

Lord, my longing is to not miss your goodness and grace.
Would you give me eyes to see, even during today, those around me
through the lens of your compassion and love for them. Amen

RUTH HASSALL

An uninvited guest

When one of the Pharisees invited Jesus to have dinner with him, he went to the Pharisee's house and reclined at the table. A woman in that town who lived a sinful life learned that Jesus was eating at the Pharisee's house, so she came there with an alabaster jar of perfume. As she stood behind him at his feet weeping, she began to wet his feet with her tears. Then she wiped them with her hair, kissed them and poured perfume on them. When the Pharisee who had invited him saw this, he said to himself, 'If this man were a prophet, he would know who is touching him and what kind of woman she is – that she is a sinner.'

It really seems that in the eyes of the Pharisees, Jesus just cannot get it right. Yesterday we saw how, in their opinion, Jesus was in the wrong house with the wrong people. Today we find him in the right house, but somehow still in the wrong company. In fact, in Luke's gospel, it was precisely because Jesus chose to eat with those considered to be outcasts that those in power challenged his authority.

For some reason, Simon the Pharisee invites Jesus to come and dine in his home. As they were at the table an uninvited woman suddenly appears and without speaking, pours out her tears and perfumed oil on Jesus' feet.

We cannot help but contrast the unnamed 'sinful' woman's lavish act of hospitality and devotion with Simon's failure to offer even the most basic of normal courtesies when Jesus arrived at his home. Was it because Simon did not really hold Jesus in any sort of regard, but was just intrigued to see if this man was really who he claimed to be – and then decided that he was not when he allowed this 'sinful' woman to approach him in that way?

This act of love led to the woman's sins being forgiven and a whole new future opening up before her. But Simon's confidence in his own righteousness kept him from recognising the gift of Jesus' presence, and the debt of love that was his.

Are you someone who is quick to respond in love
and devotion to the forgiveness you have received in Christ?

RUTH HASSALL

A surprising banquet

Jesus replied: 'A certain man was preparing a great banquet and invited many guests. At the time of the banquet he sent his servant to tell those who had been invited, "Come, for everything is now ready." But they all alike began to make excuses... The owner of the house became angry and ordered his servant, "Go out quickly into the streets and alleys of the town and bring in the poor, the crippled, the blind and the lame... Go out to the roads and country lanes and compel them to come in, so that my house will be full. I tell you, not one of those who were invited will get a taste of my banquet."'

When Jesus wanted to describe the nature of the kingdom of God, he often chose to use the image of a great banquet. Through this parable he is setting out the mission that he has before him of inviting the whole of humanity into a living relationship with God the Father. It is a relationship that none of us deserve or can possibly earn, but which comes to us as a grace-filled gift.

As the parable unfolds, we are brought face to face with the harsh reality of the human heart. In response to this wonderful banquet invitation, the original invitees find one excuse after another as to why they cannot possibly attend; too occupied with their business, their family commitments, other priorities and so the list goes on. It is not so much that they did not want to attend, there were just more important things in their lives to consider.

However, undeterred, the host (who we understand to be God himself) insists that every place be filled. If the first invited guests will not come, then those who would not normally ever find themselves listed as an honoured guest will receive an invitation to come and join the feast. The generosity of the host, the generosity of God, knows no bounds. All are welcome to sit around his table and enjoy the banquet. The only requirement? A heart that is willing to respond.

As I reflect on this passage, I am drawn to ask – how is my heart?
And how do I make known God's invitation, that all may come?

RUTH HASSALL

A meal to remember

When the hour came, Jesus and his apostles reclined at the table. And he said to them, 'I have eagerly desired to eat this Passover with you before I suffer. For I tell you, I will not eat it again until it finds fulfilment in the kingdom of God… Do this in remembrance of me.'

Last meals are significant events. People often gather with their close friends and family before they head off somewhere for a significant length of time. It is around the table that we share our stories, make memories and express our love for the ones going away and the ones left behind.

In this most significant of last meals, Jesus gathers with his friends, heart heavy with all that he knew the next few days were going to hold, and gives them an important memory to hold on to. They are celebrating a Passover meal as they would have done with their families and communities since childhood, but this time Jesus takes an old symbol and fills it with new meaning, which the apostles would not have fully grasped until later on.

In the breaking of bread and the outpouring of wine, Jesus explains that these are not just things to be taken and enjoyed, but are to serve as a reminder of his body broken and his blood shed for them. Jesus' ministry had always been about welcoming sinners and often eating with them, and in this poignant last meal, Jesus is demonstrating the full depth of what that means, and what it costs. Jesus knew that around the table was one who would betray him and one who would deny him, yet there were no caveats – his suffering would be for all, so that all can know the forgiveness of their sins and restoration of relationship with the Father.

God's love and faithfulness are seen in this simple act. Around God's table we are all on level ground, not because we deserve to be there, but because through God's grace we are invited to take our place. May we be those who always remember, and eat and drink with a deep thankfulness that Jesus chose to give himself so that we might receive his gift of love.

Lord, thank you for your ever open invitation. Thank you that you extended it to me and opened my heart to respond. May my welcome and invitation reflect the warmth of your heart for those who are on the margins. Amen

RUTH HASSALL

The unfinished meal

As they approached the village to which they were going, Jesus continued on as if he were going further. But they urged him strongly, 'Stay with us, for it is nearly evening; the day is almost over.' So he went in to stay with them. When he was at the table with them, he took bread, gave thanks, broke it and began to give it to them. Then their eyes were opened and they recognised him, and he disappeared from their sight. They asked each other, 'Were not our hearts burning within us while he talked with us on the road and opened the scriptures to us?'

As we meet these two travellers heading towards Emmaus on the road out of Jerusalem, we find that grief is doing the work that it so often does: making them question whether they could believe all that they had just heard. Their hearts were heavy with hopes that had been crushed and they were wondering what of the last few years had actually been true.

As they talk, another traveller comes alongside them and joins them in their conversation, asking them the reason for their sorrow. They are surprised that he even has to ask, but share with him the news of Jesus' death, not knowing that it is he who walks with them.

On reaching their destination, they invite Jesus to join them for a meal. The conversation continues and no doubt the questions continue to flow, but in a moment everything changes. Jesus takes the bread, blesses it and breaks it, and they realise with deep joy who their companion is. As he gives them the bread, they receive fresh hope. Their questions may not have been answered but his presence removed all their doubt. As quickly as their lives had been shattered and defeated by despair, they were now renewed and restored. The meal never gets finished – Jesus disappears and they make a quick return to Jerusalem to share this news that they cannot keep to themselves!

Still today, in the breaking of bread, Jesus makes himself known. We may not get the answers to all our questions, but the gift of his presence can quieten our minds and bring hope to our hearts.

Can you bring to mind a time recently where you have known
the closeness of God's presence in this way?

RUTH HASSALL

Breakfast on the beach

Jesus said to them, 'Bring some of the fish you have just caught.' So Simon Peter climbed back into the boat and dragged the net ashore. It was full of large fish, 153, but even with so many the net was not torn. Jesus said to them, 'Come and have breakfast.' None of the disciples dared ask him, 'Who are you?' They knew it was the Lord. Jesus came, took the bread and gave it to them, and did the same with the fish.

Much has happened for the disciples since they were gathered around that final table with Jesus. It is no wonder that Peter has returned to the comfort of the familiar routine of a former life. We can only imagine what was going through his mind as he reflected on the events of the previous days – seeing Jesus so horribly crucified, his own words of betrayal and the gradual realisation that Jesus truly was alive. And now as he comes into shore, once again he is face to face with the risen Jesus, the one he had so quickly abandoned. As Peter watched Jesus cooking him breakfast, taking bread and giving it to him, I wonder if other memories came flooding back – of the feeding of thousands on another shore or of the meal so recently shared.

In a little while Jesus would be having a conversation with Peter which, while not all together comfortable, would ultimately be the pathway to not only Peter's restoration but also his commission to love others and lead them in the way of Jesus. I really love the kindness of Jesus, that he would take the time to feed the hungry fisherman; to first offer him a breakfast made with love and care and to demonstrate there was no distance in his heart from Peter.

Peter may have felt that he had lost his direction, that he didn't know where else to turn other than the past during those difficult days. But Jesus once more draws him close and, by the warmth of the fire and with the comfort of a good breakfast, lets him know they will walk forward together.

In times of disappointment with ourselves, we too can have confidence that Jesus draws us near, even if at first we do not recognise that it is him.

RUTH HASSALL

The fellowship meal

They devoted themselves to the apostles' teaching and to fellowship, to the breaking of bread and to prayer… All the believers were together and had everything in common… Every day they continued to meet together in the temple courts. They broke bread in their homes and ate together with glad and sincere hearts, praising God and enjoying the favour of all the people. And the Lord added to their number daily those who were being saved.

The story of God's hospitality does not end with Jesus and the hope of an eternal banquet that one day we will get to attend; the story goes on in the meantime, and Luke picks it up in the stories he records in the book of Acts.

A number of commentaries debate whether the pattern set out here in Acts 2 is a blueprint for us or whether we should admit that those were unique moments in the life of the early church which are not something we can replicate in our busy lives today. Wherever we land on this debate, one thing that is clear is that hospitality is a characteristic that the Holy Spirit still inspires in God's people today.

In the age of Instagram, it is easy to think that your house needs to be perfect and your culinary ability that of a Michelin star chef before you can invite people in. But really hospitality is not about a perfect house, it is about an open, loving home: a home where people can come and be restored; know themselves welcomed and loved; and where life in God can be shared. In those homes, the simplest of food tastes rich and nourishing.

It is around the table that stories get shared and friendships are made. In these days when we are welcoming so many refugees and asylum seekers into our towns and cities, can we be people who reflect the heart of God? Can we say, 'There is always a place here for you. Come, eat and enjoy and know something of the goodness of God' – the God whose invitation is always 'Come for tea, come for tea' – and in the enjoyment of a meal, find that hearts are refreshed and drawn deeper into his love?

Lord, thank you for the fellowship of eating together. Help us welcome others as a sign of the eternal banquet to which you invite us all. Amen.

RUTH HASSALL

John 3 and 4

Chapters 3 and 4 of John's gospel describe the launch of Jesus' mission to the world. He has already gathered his disciples, thanks in part to John the Baptist's testimony, and he has performed his first miracle, on home ground in Galilee. He shows himself to be a reformer of Jewish custom and practice by cleansing the temple and is causing a stir among his people.

Chapter 2 closes with the comment: 'But Jesus on his part would not entrust himself to them [those who believed in his signs] because he knew all people and needed no one to testify about anyone, for he himself knew what was in everyone' (John 2:24–25, NRSV). This is what we see playing out in Jesus' subsequent encounters with both Nicodemus the Jewish teacher and the Samaritan woman. Jesus can read their hearts and he speaks to them with supernatural insight.

Despite Jesus' abilities, however, these encounters do not give the impression of being entirely one-sided. If there is misunderstanding, Jesus clarifies with further revelation of his divine origins and mission, in the hope that his conversation partners will see his glory. Through dialogue, Jesus seeks to establish relationship with those he meets, based on mutual personal recognition. This intimacy is eternal life: it draws the believer into the eternal bond Jesus himself has with the Father who sent him. All who receive him, therefore, have the power to become children of God (1:12).

What the stories do that the theology cannot convey is the bespoke quality of Jesus' conversation. The conversation with Nicodemus is robust and confrontational, while with the Samaritan woman it is searching and invitational. Jesus shows himself to be the human link to God, the one who knows what it is like to be a human relating to God and a human relating to others in and through the same mortal flesh.

These conversations are always more than individual. They segue into editorial comments made by the evangelist which draw out their significance. There are not only changes from the singular to the plural 'you', which suddenly address a wider audience, but there are also changes into the present tense, where readers and hearers are addressed directly and given the chance to believe in this Jesus for themselves.

ROLAND RIEM

Jesus the teacher

Jesus answered him, 'Very truly, I tell you, no one can see the kingdom of God without being born from above.' Nicodemus said to him, 'How can anyone be born after having grown old? Can one enter a second time into the mother's womb and be born?' Jesus answered, 'Very truly, I tell you, no one can enter the kingdom of God without being born of water and Spirit. What is born of the flesh is flesh, and what is born of the Spirit is spirit. Do not be astonished that I said to you, "You must be born from above."'

For a teacher, a misunderstanding can be useful, because it allows for clarification and opens the way to a fuller insight. This applies whether the misunderstanding comes from a first-century Pharisee like Nicodemus or from ourselves, the present readers.

Nicodemus seeks Jesus out secretly 'by night' (John 3:2). He politely acknowledges him as a rabbi, a teacher from God. But even before he asks a question, the teacher knows what Nicodemus needs to find – a way into God's kingdom. A Pharisee would have thought that this would be achieved by fulfilling God's commandments, not by being 'born anew' in any way, shape or form. It is no surprise that Nicodemus gets tangled up with thoughts of a second physical birth. Jesus the teacher confronts this misunderstanding with a clear distinction between flesh and Spirit. The realm 'above' is the realm of Spirit. It is not the realm of the flesh, the realm of human endeavour, but the realm of the supernatural where God's initiative rules.

Keeping the law was never Jesus' way into God's kingdom. That is apparent to anyone looking at how Jesus lived. He did not follow the conventions of how the law was interpreted and defended, and he paid the highest price for his Spirit-filled freedom.

If we look for an external standard to produce a life of freedom and fruitfulness, we shall find Jesus' words as baffling as Nicodemus did. Being born again is a radical turn, rooting ourselves far above the human humdrum. To enter God's kingdom, we must start where God dwells, in the realm of Spirit, the giver and constant refashioner of life.

Lord, bring me to birth once more in the realm of Spirit. Amen

ROLAND RIEM

The known unknown

'The wind blows where it chooses, and you hear the sound of it, but you do not know where it comes from or where it goes. So it is with everyone who is born of the Spirit.' Nicodemus said to him, 'How can these things be?' Jesus answered him, 'Are you the teacher of Israel, and yet you do not understand these things? Very truly, I tell you, we speak of what we know and testify to what we have seen; yet you do not receive our testimony.'

The realm of the Spirit is a mysterious realm, completely unlike the familiar realm of the flesh. How can we even to begin to understand it? Jesus gives Nicodemus the simplest of images to contemplate: the sound of the wind.

The association of God's Spirit with wind goes back to the very opening of the Bible, with God's wind sweeping over the surface of the waters (Genesis 1:2). Jesus, however, personifies the wind, giving it the choice over where it blows. This turns a simple image into something mysterious, suggesting that we are always catching up on how the Spirit has already chosen to act. We only hear the echo of an ever-gusting Spirit.

Yet this Spirit need not remain remote from our human being; it is possible to come to know the drama of the wind inwardly, but not without being completely remade – born again. Being reborn means a completely new beginning, a reconfiguring of our hard drive, by the working of the Spirit.

Nicodemus really does not understand, and Jesus, who has been seeking to reveal the truth to Nicodemus, is naturally disappointed with a teacher who will not learn. All Jesus can do is solemnly assure Nicodemus that he knows these truths firsthand, under the impulse of the Spirit. It is the Spirit who is causing him to speak as boldly and directly as he does.

As those born of the Spirit, we too will speak boldly of what we inwardly know, though we should be careful not to claim too much for ourselves. It is easy to swap what the ever-free Spirit chooses to do through us, and what we might have an inkling of knowing, for an idol of our own imagination.

Not claiming too much, let us be claimed by you. Amen

ROLAND RIEM

Bridging the gap

'If I have told you about earthly things and you do not believe, how can you believe if I tell you about heavenly things? No one has ascended into heaven except the one who descended from heaven, the Son of Man. And just as Moses lifted up the serpent in the wilderness, so must the Son of Man be lifted up, that whoever believes in him may have eternal life.'

The gap between the realms of flesh and Spirit seems impossible to bridge, and yet John's gospel tells exactly that story: Jesus is sent by God to bridge the gap, so that the realm of the Spirit above can be known intimately in the flesh.

Nicodemus, though he fails to understand, is presented with a lesson in how God draws close. Jesus translates spiritual realities into earthly experiences like hearing the wind, so that not only Nicodemus but everyone may know where God is coming from and how to join his work. In the English translation, we do not hear the shift from the singular to the plural form of 'you'. However, once Jesus has challenged Nicodemus specifically, his words fill a wider stage – the 'you' being taught heavenly things is plural.

The lesson about serpents comes from the book of Numbers in the Old Testament, where the Lord told Moses to fashion a bronze serpent to cure those bitten by poisonous snakes in the wilderness. The people had to face what they most feared, a horrible death. Jesus' death in John's gospel is not portrayed as an anguished one, because it reveals a victory over the power of death. Jesus' serenity on the cross is a sign of God's antidote to the poison of death, which only Christ can offer.

The detail that the Son of Man must be 'lifted up' accentuates the truth that our salvation is achieved by Jesus returning from the world below to heaven above. And Jesus being lifted up in public display accentuates the truth that this salvation is a universal gift from God to all who believe in him.

We are saved not by avoiding death but by believing in the one who faced and overcame death gloriously as he was lifted up high on the cross.

Look up to the crucified one to see death defeated.

ROLAND RIEM

God's final offer

'For God so loved the world that he gave his only Son, so that everyone who believes in him may not perish but may have eternal life. Indeed, God did not send the Son into the world to condemn the world but in order that the world might be saved through him.'

There is a way of telling the story of God which sets God in a pure, unapproachable light, so that in his absolute holiness God has to wear a mask in order to deal with the virus of human sin without being put at risk. In this, somewhat skewed, telling of the gospel, the ultra-holy God can only deal with the world's darkness through Jesus, whom he sends to deal at a distance with our contamination.

The most famous verse in the Bible, John 3:16, sets the record straight about salvation and it is spoken once Nicodemus has faded from the scene and John the Evangelist is addressing his readers directly.

Salvation begins with God loving the world, to such an extent that the Father is prepared to enter in a new way into the life of the world through his only Son Jesus – a way that goes beyond the law, the prophets, the kings and the judges whom he had previously raised up to deliver his people.

This costly identification with the world constitutes God's final offer, because after Jesus God has nothing left to give. There is no other Son hiding in the wings to do a better job for God; quite the contrary, it is only Jesus who in his person has the life of an eternal child of God to offer us.

We do not believe that God is Trinity to provoke the other great monotheistic faiths: we hold that God is Father, Son and Holy Spirit because in those eternal relationships lie our salvation. We are drawn into the love of the Father through Jesus Christ by the grace of the Spirit.

In Jesus God has entered the world he has made with total commitment, to offer us the very heart of his eternal, loving life. And anyone, absolutely anyone, who believes in Jesus has the right to receive that life and be saved.

Lord, we open our hands and heart to your gift. Amen

ROLAND RIEM

The lesser light

They came to John and said to him, 'Rabbi, the one who was with you across the Jordan, to whom you testified, here he is baptising, and all are going to him.' John answered, 'No one can receive anything except what has been given from heaven. You yourselves are my witnesses that I said, "I am not the Messiah, but I have been sent ahead of him." He who has the bride is the bridegroom. The friend of the bridegroom who stands and hears him rejoices greatly at the bridegroom's voice. For this reason my joy has been fulfilled. He must increase, but I must decrease.'

The relationship of Jesus to John the Baptist was a matter of contention as the gospel was being completed. It left its mark right from the beginning, where the prologue is interrupted by a man sent by God as a witness to testify to the light of Jesus – someone who, we hear, was not himself the light.

John's disciples may have felt themselves to be in competition with Jesus', but John himself meets their performance anxiety with some steady words about his relationship to Jesus. He is not the Messiah who is coming as a bridegroom to claim his bride, his community, but more like a 'best man', who in Jewish ceremony had the role of leading the bride to the bridegroom.

With this competitive backdrop it is especially striking that John the Baptist's last words in this gospel are, 'He must increase, but I must decrease' (v. 30). Unlike Nicodemus, who simply fades from the scene, the Baptist bows out gracefully. He has done exactly what he has been called to do, namely, to make way for the one who is greater. And the sign of his obedience is his joy.

John rejoices at the bridegroom's voice. He hears its authenticity, speaking only what has been given from heaven. He hears the voice of the lamb of God who will achieve a baptism more definitive than his own.

Similarly, our hope as disciples will be to play a small part in God's story and, at the right time, to give way gracefully and joyfully to whoever we hear and see building on our own small contribution.

Not to us, Lord, but to your name alone be the glory. Amen

ROLAND RIEM

Judgement from heaven

The one who comes from above is above all; the one who is of the earth belongs to the earth and speaks about earthly things. The one who comes from heaven is above all. He testifies to what he has seen and heard, yet no one accepts his testimony. Whoever has accepted his testimony has certified this, that God is true. He whom God has sent speaks the words of God, for he gives the Spirit without measure. The Father loves the Son and has placed all things in his hands. Whoever believes in the Son has eternal life; whoever disobeys the Son will not see life but must endure God's wrath.

Chapter 3 ends with some further commentary from the Evangelist about the gulf between the realm above and the realm below, this time called the earth rather than the flesh, giving the ordinary a wider scope.

The gospel was not written to promote God's glory as an abstract quality, or to put Jesus on a pedestal; it was written so that through believing that Jesus is the Messiah we might have life in his name (see John 20:31). If anything is said about God and revealed about God, it is done for our benefit.

Nicodemus missed the point, while John the Baptist got it completely. The Evangelist steps forward to drive home the message that the Father has sent the Son, who speaks through the Spirit, and that this is the way in which we are offered eternal life. There are only two directions to travel in relation to this economy of salvation, either towards belief or towards disobedience, that is, a wilful disbelief.

For faithful followers of Jesus, it doesn't always feel as if we are making this choice in our daily, earthly existence. We get stuck on an earthly level, fearing to look 'up' from our preoccupations. Our wilful ignorance risks God's wrath, as he contends for our attention and repentance.

But belief means turning in trust to the Messiah, who brings grace into our ordinary, sometimes compromised, everyday lives to reveal the Father's love and to take us into that love by making us his children also.

The greatest disobedience is to reject love.

ROLAND RIEM

The woman at the well

Now when Jesus learned that the Pharisees had heard, 'Jesus is making and baptising more disciples than John' (although it was not Jesus himself but his disciples who baptised), he left Judea and started back to Galilee. But he had to go through Samaria. So he came to a Samaritan city called Sychar, near the plot of ground that Jacob had given to his son Joseph. Jacob's well was there, and Jesus, tired out by his journey, was sitting by the well. It was about noon.

At one level Jesus moves away from Judea because he wants to avoid confrontation with the Pharisees there; on another level, he moves north through Samaria because he 'has to': he is impelled by the wind of the Spirit to pass through the home of the Samaritans. There was an alternative route back to Galilee, but this was not God's appointed way.

We know that Samaritans came to be despised by their Jewish cousins, and so this coming meeting with an unnamed Samaritan woman with a tangled history contrasts very markedly with the meeting Jesus had with the respected Jewish leader Nicodemus, whose name we do know. We see in the meeting with this woman, who comes to him in the midday heat, rather than by night as Nicodemus had, something of the universal reach of God's only Son.

The common religious ancestry held by the Samaritan and Jewish people was the patriarchs. A meeting by the patriarch Jacob's well, therefore, was very significant, as this spot belonged to both traditions. Everything in this brief introduction hints at God's providence in this moment and the prospect of Jesus bringing together alienated peoples into a shared community of faith.

Jesus' being worn out, and thus sitting down at the well to rest in the full heat of the day, gives us a sense of the humanity with which he will engage with the Samaritan woman. Though his words come from above, he never talks down to people from on high, and his desire to speak for the Father who sent him never displaces his desire to reach out in compassion to those who, like him, hunger and thirst. And that includes us all.

We cannot despise our need if Christ shares it with us.

ROLAND RIEM

Living water

The woman said to him, 'Sir, you have no bucket, and the well is deep. Where do you get that living water? Are you greater than our ancestor Jacob, who gave us the well and with his sons and his flocks drank from it?' Jesus said to her, 'Everyone who drinks of this water will be thirsty again, but those who drink of the water that I will give them will never be thirsty. The water that I will give will become in them a spring of water gushing up to eternal life.'

The Samaritan woman who comes to the well is astonished by Jesus. That he should ask her for a drink is surprise enough, but then he offers more: the gift of living water. As with Nicodemus, there is room in this conversation for misunderstanding, because 'living' water can mean 'running' water. And once again, just as we heard earlier of the wind blowing where it wills, so we have here a spring of water gushing up – natural images pointing to supernatural truths. The water given by Jesus is unique because it will be a spring gushing up to eternal life: it is water that will bring salvation.

The woman replies, 'Sir, give me this water, so that I may never be thirsty or have to keep coming here to draw water' (v. 15). The issue remains of thirst and the wearisome trudge that coming to get water invokes, made harder for her by being a social outcast. This gushing spring would change her life completely.

This outsider has moved a long way through her misunderstanding over the water Jesus offers from God. Astonishment has given way to curiosity. And however much Jesus will challenge this thirsty woman in what follows, he will never deny her fundamental desire for a freer, fuller life.

Jesus' mission is not only to reveal himself as being at one with the Father but also to reveal the complexities of the human heart. For her and for all of us, Jesus wants to reach through this real knottiness to get to the bottom of our thirst, and to plunge deeper still into its wellsprings of hope. To him all desires are known and no secrets are hidden.

Cleanse the thoughts of our hearts; revive our parched souls. Amen

ROLAND RIEM

The truth emerges

Jesus said to her, 'Go, call your husband, and come back.' The woman answered him, 'I have no husband.' Jesus said to her, 'You are right in saying, "I have no husband," for you have had five husbands, and the one you have now is not your husband. What you have said is true!' The woman said to him, 'Sir, I see that you are a prophet. Our ancestors worshipped on this mountain, but you say that the place where people must worship is in Jerusalem.' Jesus said to her, 'Woman, believe me, the hour is coming when you will worship the Father neither on this mountain nor in Jerusalem. You worship what you do not know; we worship what we know, for salvation is from the Jews.'

This part of the conversation between Jesus and the Samaritan woman feels like a dance into truth. It is also what God's judgement looks like, as Jesus strips back the layers of this woman's self-defence and self-definition to reveal a purer, plainer image beneath. Once she has dared to admit the truth that she has no husband, Jesus shows her how deeply he knows her. To Christ she is no anonymous outsider.

Having honoured Jesus as a prophet, the woman turns to the differences in their religious traditions – whether to evade or engage him, perhaps both. But Jesus responds by drawing her to the core issue, which is not about where God is worshipped, which divides them, but about how God is known, which may yet come to unite them.

At this point in the story, the gospel crosses from past to future present and from singular to plural, because what started as a conversation between two people ends as a proclamation of eternal and universal truth: 'You [all] worship what you do not know' (v. 22), but Jesus the Jew worships what he does know, and this Jesus opens the way to salvation for all who do not yet know it.

The temple in Jerusalem was destroyed in AD70, before this gospel was written, but the salvation which is from the Jews, now relocated in the temple which is his risen body, remains ours and everyone else's in Christ.

Christ's risen body: the resting place for all people and nations.

ROLAND RIEM

In spirit now

But the hour is coming and is now here when the true worshippers will worship the Father in spirit and truth, for the Father seeks such as these to worship him. God is spirit, and those who worship him must worship in spirit and truth.' The woman said to him, 'I know that Messiah is coming' (who is called Christ). 'When he comes, he will proclaim all things to us.' Jesus said to her, 'I am he, the one who is speaking to you.'

In the preceding conversation when Jesus said to the woman, 'The hour is coming when you will worship', the hour seemed sometime in the future. However, the perspective shifts further as he continues, 'The hour is coming, and is now here.' The future has arrived. Jesus says this to open to the woman the new possibilities before her as he sits beside her.

An analogy may help here. We know about black holes: they are objects so dense that their gravity bends the space-time continuum so that not even light can escape. Space and time are affected profoundly by this super-dense object, which turns out to be the very opposite of a hole. And so it is with Jesus: as he reveals to the woman and to future believers the density of his divine being, his I-AM-ness present in their midst disrupts the ordinary flow of space and time. In this I AM made flesh, true worship is now possible.

For the woman and for all listening to this encounter, worship in spirit and in truth begins now in Jesus. The location for this worship is neither in Jerusalem nor on Mount Gerizim but is in Jesus himself as he reveals himself as God's Word, the one whose speech draws all who receive it into the heart of the Father.

Worship in spirit and truth, then, happens naturally through opening oneself to Jesus, the bearer of the Spirit who proclaims all things to us truthfully in a way that we can accept, gradually and mindful of our hesitations. What he says to each of us will take us on a journey into truths we can hardly perceive or imagine but which in him already find their full expression.

Not knowing it all already is what makes the adventure.

ROLAND RIEM

The end of food and drink

Just then his disciples came. They were astonished that he was speaking with a woman, but no one said, 'What do you want?' or, 'Why are you speaking with her?' Then the woman left her water jar and went back to the city. She said to the people, 'Come and see a man who told me everything I have ever done! He cannot be the Messiah, can he?' They left the city and were on their way to him. Meanwhile the disciples were urging him, 'Rabbi, eat something.' But he said to them, 'I have food to eat that you do not know about.' So the disciples said to one another, 'Surely no one has brought him something to eat?' Jesus said to them, 'My food is to do the will of him who sent me and to complete his work.'

The conversation with the Samaritan woman is bracketed between the disciples leaving for food and coming back with it. As they return, they are naturally shocked to see Jesus speaking to a woman alone. Equally naturally, they do not dare to challenge him about it.

The unnamed woman returns to her people, leaving her bucket behind, no longer locked in the cycle of thirst from which she was hoping to escape. Though she will need to drink water again, she is now living for a higher purpose.

She has become a witness to Christ. She testifies to him just as she has received him, as a man unafraid to meet her, who has shown himself to fully know her. Salvation works not by God imposing his glory on us but by Jesus establishing a personal, gentle relationship with us through his outstretched humanity.

The woman's witness to Jesus' grace and truth enveloping her is tentative but authentic. She proclaims as much as she knows and all that she hopes, which is enough to move her whole city towards faith in the Messiah.

The disciples, meanwhile, urge food on Jesus, which leads to misunderstanding from them this time. So Jesus begins to teach his disciples with food what he has just taught the woman with water: their claims about hunger are less essential than fulfilling God's eternal will, even amidst all our pressing human needs and desires.

No need is greater than to be fully God's.

ROLAND RIEM

Labouring in abundance

'Do you not say, "Four months more, then comes the harvest"? But I tell you, look around you, and see how the fields are ripe for harvesting. The reaper is already receiving wages and is gathering fruit for eternal life, so that sower and reaper may rejoice together. For here the saying holds true, "One sows and another reaps." I sent you to reap that for which you did not labour. Others have laboured, and you have entered into their labour.'

'The hour is coming and is now here', said Jesus to the Samaritan woman as he sat beside her. In him the future has already arrived. But that is not all there is to be said about what has now been made present through Jesus, because as God's Messiah, Jesus ushers in a new age.

This is what Jesus wants his disciples to understand as they stand before him perplexed at his rejecting their offer of food. Food is produced by the cycle of human labour and through the patience of waiting for crops to grow before harvesting. In rejecting food, Jesus turns the imagination of the disciples to a different kind of harvest and a different perspective on time.

In this new age of abundance, the sower and reaper are rejoicing together: the Father who sent Jesus into the world and Jesus who is already receiving from the Father the wages of obedient service and gathering fruit for eternal life. This is what those with eyes to see will find in the story of the Samaritan woman leaving without her bucket, and her city making their way to seek him.

Jesus is doing more than pointing out what the Father is doing through the Son, however much it may rejoice the heart of God to see this in-gathering. He is inviting his disciples to share in the work, 'reaping for that for which they did not labour'.

The life of a disciple is not easy, for we cannot follow our own will, even our more positive aspirations, but it will be disproportionately fruitful as we do the will of the one who sent us. The effort will be collaborative, with Jesus and with all others who feel a new dawn breaking.

Where are those kingdom-moments of unexpected abundance?

ROLAND RIEM

Dwelling time

Many Samaritans from that city believed in him because of the woman's testimony, 'He told me everything I have ever done.' So when the Samaritans came to him, they asked him to stay with them, and he stayed there two days. And many more believed because of his word. They said to the woman, 'It is no longer because of what you said that we believe, for we have heard for ourselves, and we know that this is truly the Saviour of the world.'

What does the promised spring of water gushing up to eternal life look like? It looks like a fountain of joyful commitment, springing from the heart of God and drawing many people into its flow. This is what happens as many Samaritans become real disciples who believe in Jesus for themselves.

This story echoes the calling of the first disciples, who turned to Jesus because of the testimony of John the Baptist. Here it is the woman who points the way to her people, witnessing to Jesus' prophetic understanding of her life story. And like the first disciples, who asked Jesus where he was staying and remained with him one day, so these Samaritans also approach Jesus with a request to stay with him, even remaining a day longer than the disciples did.

There are two further signs that these Samaritans are fully committed to Christ: the first disciples called him Rabbi and then Messiah; these Samaritan disciples confess Jesus as 'the Saviour of the world', a more universal and exalted title. Furthermore, the Samaritans bear witness that they believe because they have heard God's word for themselves, a word that addresses them as completely as Jesus' bold words to the woman. Their believing is more than a mere alignment to Jesus' message; it is a joyful recognition and acceptance that in Jesus they are known and accepted as belonging to God. Jesus is Saviour of the world because he saves Jew and Samaritan alike.

The story will go on to include a royal official receiving healing for his son, who may or may not have been a Gentile. Jesus carries on breaking the boundaries of salvation, until he comes to us and stretches those boundaries even further.

God, we have heard, believed and rejoice in your word. Amen

ROLAND RIEM

Back to Galilee

He went from that place to Galilee (for Jesus himself had testified that a prophet has no honour in the prophet's own country). When he came to Galilee, the Galileans welcomed him, since they had seen all that he had done in Jerusalem at the festival, for they, too, had gone to the festival. Then he came again to Cana in Galilee, where he had changed the water into wine. Now there was a royal official whose son lay ill in Capernaum. When he heard that Jesus had come from Judea to Galilee, he went and begged him to come down and heal his son, for he was at the point of death.

Jesus returns to Galilee, his own region. This small and puzzling interlude in the gospel after the evident success of the Samaritan mission links with the end of John 2. There Jesus' kinsfolk were with him at the Jerusalem festival, and 'many believed in his name because they saw the signs he was doing' (2:23), but Jesus did not entrust himself to them.

That was wise. Nicodemus' dialogue with Jesus underlines how being attracted to Jesus' signs is not genuine belief. Neither Nicodemus nor the crowds get to the point at which they stay with Jesus, which is where Jesus leaves the Samaritans. The problem, as Jesus himself testifies, is that it is very hard to be seen for who you are on your own home patch.

The problem is not territorial; today's passage continues in Cana in Galilee, with one of the most startling stories of faith in the gospel. The irony is that the one who completely trusts Jesus' authority is a royal official who is very unlikely to have been Jewish. On the other hand, Jesus' kinsfolk think they know who he is and so are unprepared to receive his everlasting gift: 'He came to what was his own, and his own people did not accept him' (John 1:11).

It is very easy for faithful people to close themselves off from the life-giving gift of Jesus. He becomes too familiar to us. Admiring Jesus or being entranced by features of his ministry cannot in themselves plunge us into the wellspring of salvation. For that we need to seek the Christ who we do not yet know or fully accept.

Father, draw us to a deeper knowledge of your Son,
our light and life. Amen

Elijah: prophet of the true God

During this fortnight we journey with Elijah through highs and lows as he stands for the one true God. God's people have turned from serving and honouring him only and instead have followed Baal, the fertility god. Their hearts have been swayed by that god's promises of teeming abundance, which, when God sends a drought for three years, are shown to be as worthless as a dried-up piece of grass.

We can gain much from this prophet's story, even if showdowns over sacrifices seem far removed from us today. We see Elijah's faith in God grow and solidify as he trusts God through the drought, as he is sent provisions through the weakest in society and as he stands against the evil king and his wife. We also witness the prophet's plummeting into despair after his great victory. He has spent his reserves, and the journey is all too much for him. How God cares for his needs so tenderly is a beloved story in the Old Testament that gives us hope and encouragement when we too feel physically and emotionally spent. Elijah has been used by God for great things, but he reveals his limitations and frailty after the big confrontation with the prophets of Baal.

We can find hope when Elijah passes on the mantle of his office to Elisha. When he tells God that he wants out from this harried and difficult life, God sends him his successor and they then get to work together. Elijah finds companionship in the lonely work of one called to defend the name and honour of God.

I pray you will be encouraged by this story of an ordinary person called to do extraordinary things. He displays great faith, but he also dips in his belief of God. Yet God does not write him off. So too does God deal with us gently. He sends us provisions when we need them and speaks to us in a quiet whisper. He gives us colleagues to share the tasks before us. In short, he never gives up on us.

May we share Elijah's belief that God will deliver when we face hardship; may we honour and serve God and God only, just as this prophet did so many years ago.

AMY BOUCHER PYE

The Lord is God

Now Elijah the Tishbite, from Tishbe in Gilead, said to Ahab, 'As the Lord, the God of Israel, lives, whom I serve, there will be neither dew nor rain in the next few years except at my word.' Then the word of the Lord came to Elijah: 'Leave here, turn eastward and hide in the Kerith Ravine, east of the Jordan. You will drink from the brook, and I have instructed the ravens to supply you with food there.' So he did what the Lord had told him… The ravens brought him bread and meat in the morning and bread and meat in the evening, and he drank from the brook.

Bursting on to the scene is Elijah, a prophet who declares the power of God even through his name, which means 'My God is the Lord.' From the descriptor we learn that he is an immigrant to the northern kingdom of Israel. He appears in response to the apostasy of King Ahab of Israel, who 'did more evil in the eyes of the Lord than any of those before him' (1 Kings 16:30).

Elijah pronounces not only that he serves God but also that they are entering a period of drought. He is throwing down the gauntlet against Baal, the god Ahab serves, who is a fertility god. Those who follow Baal believe that each year he must die in order to bring back the healing rains. Thus by saying that no rain will come unless he directs it, Elijah declares to Ahab: 'Bring it on! Let's see who is more powerful.'

The Lord telling Elijah to go to the Kerith Ravine would have felt counterintuitive to him, as that river only flowed during the rainy season. And ravens were scavengers, not providers. Thus Elijah needed to trust that God really would care for him.

And God did – each morning and evening Elijah ate bread and meat and drank from the brook. These years of drought served to build the faith of Elijah, preparing him for what was to come.

As we, like Elijah, follow and serve God, he provides for us.

Lord God, help me to trust you even when I sense you leading me in ways that I wouldn't naturally choose.

AMY BOUCHER PYE

The God who provides

Then the word of the Lord came to him: 'Go at once to Zarephath in the region of Sidon and stay there. I have instructed a widow there to supply you with food'… 'As surely as the Lord your God lives,' [the widow] replied, 'I don't have any bread – only a handful of flour in a jar and a little olive oil in a jug. I am gathering a few sticks to take home and make a meal for myself and my son, that we may eat it – and die.' Elijah said to her, 'Don't be afraid. Go home and do as you have said. But first make a small loaf of bread for me from what you have and bring it to me, and then make something for yourself and your son. For this is what the Lord, the God of Israel, says: "The jar of flour will not be used up and the jug of oil will not run dry until the day the Lord sends rain on the land."'

Elijah experiences more counterintuitive instructions from God when the brook dries up, namely to go and find a widow, the most vulnerable in that society, for food and water. Where God sends Elijah is instructive as well, for the father of Ahab's wife lives and rules in Zarephath: God directs Elijah right into the bastion of Baal worship.

During these dire times, not only Elijah but also this widow, who is not an Israelite, must trust God. Even with the drought so severe, she agrees to share her meagre provisions with the prophet, as hospitality is a strong force in her society. God stretches her resources: the jar of flour does not run out and the jug of oil does not dry up for days and days, not only for Elijah but for her and her family.

God called Elijah and this widow to trust in him, and he continues to call his people to put their faith in him today. What miraculous provision do you need? When we are faced with seemingly insurmountable challenges, we can also look back to trace where God has come through for us, sometimes in ways we can only attribute to him. May we be those who trust in him.

Lord, build my faith and belief in you; help me to look to you to provide.

AMY BOUCHER PYE

A man of God

She said to Elijah, 'What do you have against me, man of God? Did you come to remind me of my sin and kill my son?' 'Give me your son,' Elijah replied. He took him from her arms, carried him to the upper room where he was staying, and laid him on his bed. Then he cried out to the Lord, 'Lord my God, have you brought tragedy even on this widow I am staying with, by causing her son to die?' Then he stretched himself out on the boy three times and cried out to the Lord, 'Lord my God, let this boy's life return to him!' The Lord heard Elijah's cry, and the boy's life returned to him, and he lived… Then the woman said to Elijah, 'Now I know that you are a man of God and that the word of the Lord from your mouth is the truth.'

We come to a perplexing part of the story, when the widow who had been sheltering Elijah suffers a tragedy – her son dies. She immediately points to the prophet, blaming him. He also wonders why the Lord would allow this calamity and takes action.

As you consider what he does, remember that the purity laws would prevent someone from touching a dead body; in doing so they would become unclean. Elijah not only touches the boy but carries him to his room, therefore contaminating himself and his lodgings. He looks to God for help, praying with his body. And God answers, bringing restoration. This is the first instance in scripture of God raising someone from the dead – but, of course, not the last.

With this miracle, the woman believes that Elijah is a man of God, and Elijah's faith is enlarged too. He faces tragedy and feels responsible, but he looks to God who delivers him. God, not Baal, is the giver of life.

Whatever challenges we have before us, we too can put our trust whole-heartedly in God, who loves us and will answer our prayers according to his mercy and grace.

Loving God, bring restoration in my life
in the areas where the stench of death has settled.
I ask for hope and new life.

AMY BOUCHER PYE

True allegiance

After a long time, in the third year, the word of the Lord came to Elijah: 'Go and present yourself to Ahab, and I will send rain on the land'… As Obadiah was walking along, Elijah met him. Obadiah recognised him, bowed down to the ground, and said, 'Is it really you, my lord Elijah?' 'Yes,' he replied. 'Go tell your master, "Elijah is here."' 'What have I done wrong,' asked Obadiah, 'that you are handing your servant over to Ahab to be put to death? As surely as the Lord your God lives, there is not a nation or kingdom where my master has not sent someone to look for you. And whenever a nation or kingdom claimed you were not there, he made them swear they could not find you… And now you tell me to go to my master and say, "Elijah is here." He will kill me!' Elijah said, 'As the Lord Almighty lives, whom I serve, I will surely present myself to Ahab today.'

How long the three years of drought must have felt to the people of Israel. Also for Elijah, as he stays away from the evil king. Ahab keeps pursuing him while also following the orders of his wife, Jezebel, to kill the prophets. Finally God relents and promises to send some rain.

We meet Obadiah, a believer in God whose name means 'servant of Yahweh'. But he is torn, living a double life because he is the chief adviser to Ahab; for instance he saves by stealth 100 prophets of the Lord. He is wracked with anxiety, fearing that he will be the fall guy when he tells the king that Elijah has returned. Unlike the widow, who initially was not a believer in God but who obeyed, this man of faith seems to be led by fear.

Ahab seems to be more concerned with animals than people – he is off looking for grass for the horses and mules (v. 5). His misplaced priorities reveal themselves through his actions. In times of crisis, such as the disaster of drought the Israelites endured, we might be tempted to hedge our bets, dividing our trust between the things of heaven and the things of earth. We can ask God to help us look to him for our help and salvation.

Loving God, I want not to be divided in my loyalties.
Help me to honour and serve you.

AMY BOUCHER PYE

One true God

Elijah went before the people and said, 'How long will you waver between two opinions? If the Lord is God, follow him; but if Baal is God, follow him.' But the people said nothing. Then Elijah said to them, 'I am the only one of the Lord's prophets left, but Baal has four hundred and fifty prophets. Get two bulls for us. Let Baal's prophets choose one for themselves, and let them cut it into pieces and put it on the wood but not set fire to it. I will prepare the other bull and put it on the wood but not set fire to it. Then you call on the name of your god, and I will call on the name of the Lord. The god who answers by fire – he is God.' Then all the people said, 'What you say is good'… So [the prophets of Baal] took the bull that was given to them and prepared it. Then they called on the name of Baal from morning till noon. 'Baal, answer us!' they shouted. But there was no response.

We come to the showdown. God has been preparing Elijah for this confrontation all through the drought as he has kept him safe and provided for. Now Elijah's faith is put to the test as he calls on the prophets of Baal to reveal how good their god is compared with the one true God. He has bulls on the one side of him and the hundreds of prophets of Baal and Asherah on the other. By fire the living God will be revealed.

I wonder what mixture of emotions Elijah feels as he watches the prophets seeking Baal. At first they call on their god from morning to noon, to no avail. Elijah clearly enjoys their futile actions as he mocks them, their cries to Baal turning into a frenzy, including self-mutilation (v. 28). Nothing will bring forth their god.

We might pity those who worship Baal, but we can search our hearts for how we trust things other than God. For instance, how often do we rely on our financial resources, our family or community networks, our accomplishments or any other host of things in place of God? Spend a few moments asking God to show you if and how you can rely on him more fully.

Lord, I affirm that you are the one true God.
Help me to serve and honour you only.

AMY BOUCHER PYE

God of fire

He repaired the altar of the Lord, which had been torn down... Then he said to them, 'Fill four large jars with water and pour it on the offering and on the wood.' 'Do it again,' he said, and they did it again. 'Do it a third time,' he ordered, and they did it the third time... At the time of sacrifice, the prophet Elijah stepped forward and prayed... 'Answer me, Lord, answer me, so these people will know that you, Lord, are God, and that you are turning their hearts back again.' Then the fire of the Lord fell and burned up the sacrifice, the wood, the stones and the soil, and also licked up the water in the trench. When all the people saw this, they fell prostrate and cried, 'The Lord – he is God! The Lord – he is God!' Then Elijah commanded them, 'Seize the prophets of Baal. Don't let anyone get away!'

Although Elijah gave the prophets of Baal the advantage in going first, he moves ahead in faith after their failure. He signals the true worship of God as he repairs the altar and sets up twelve stones to symbolise the tribes of Israel, reminding God's people of their heritage. Such is his faith in God that he soaks the bull and the surrounding trench not once but three times. When God appears in the fire, the people will have no doubt that God is the source.

I love the simple prayer of Elijah in contrast to the frenzy of the Baal prophets. He merely states what he longs to happen – that God would make himself known – and then stands back as God answers immediately. And the people believe.

We sometimes tie ourselves up in knots as we pray, thinking we need to get it right according to what other Christians pray. But as we see in this story, God longs for a relationship with his people. As we give him honour and praise, we can also present our requests to him. He will delight to answer us.

God of fire, thank you for this story of how you made yourself known
so spectacularly. Increase my love for you,
that I may share everything with you.

AMY BOUCHER PYE

Perseverance in prayer

Elijah said to Ahab, 'Go, eat and drink, for there is the sound of a heavy rain'… Elijah climbed to the top of Carmel, bent down to the ground and put his face between his knees. 'Go and look towards the sea,' he told his servant… 'There is nothing there,' he said. Seven times Elijah said, 'Go back.' The seventh time the servant reported, 'A cloud as small as a man's hand is rising from the sea.' So Elijah said, 'Go and tell Ahab, "Hitch up your chariot and go down before the rain stops you."' Meanwhile, the sky grew black with clouds, the wind rose, a heavy rainstorm came on and Ahab rode off to Jezreel. The power of the Lord came on Elijah and, tucking his cloak into his belt, he ran ahead of Ahab all the way to Jezreel.

Elijah is a person of faith and prayer. He has seen God's power in licking up every last bit of bull and water in the trenches, and now he believes that God will send the promised rain. The drought will be over and God will be known as the true God, the real rainmaker.

Whereas yesterday we saw Elijah's simple prayer of faith, today he gives us another example of how to pray – with perseverance. He knows God will answer as he involves his body in his prayers. He goes up to the top of the mountain and then bends down as he offers his prayer and awaits God's response.

We don't sense any anxiety in the waiting. The seven times he asks the servant to check could indicate a full cycle of prayer, as seven is a special number in the Bible.

Then God responds. The small cloud is enough of a signal to Elijah for him to believe that the rains will come, and he acts accordingly as he runs to Jezreel, a journey of 17 miles.

Here Elijah is a model of faith and belief. We will see another side to him tomorrow, but here he displays grace, action and wisdom.

Faithful God, you send the rain to water the earth.
Please care for your creation, of which in so many places
we have made such a mess.

AMY BOUCHER PYE

Eat and sleep

Elijah was afraid and ran for his life. When he came to Beersheba in Judah, he left his servant there, while he himself went a day's journey into the wilderness. He came to a broom bush, sat down under it and prayed that he might die. 'I have had enough, Lord,' he said. 'Take my life; I am no better than my ancestors.' Then he lay down under the bush and fell asleep. All at once an angel touched him and said, 'Get up and eat.' He looked around, and there by his head was some bread baked over hot coals, and a jar of water. He ate and drank and then lay down again. The angel of the Lord came back a second time and touched him and said, 'Get up and eat, for the journey is too much for you.'

After the big victory comes a crash. With Jezebel issuing murderous threats against him, Elijah goes on the run. We note that he is alone – he sends his servant away – and he goes into the wilderness, which in the Bible can be a place of danger and isolation. Although Elijah has displayed great faith in the battle of the bulls, here he crashes emotionally. He is spent, and no doubt the 17-mile run has depleted him physically too.

This passage is a favourite of so many, myself included. It shows God's mercy and love in such practical ways as God takes into account Elijah's frailties. God does not ask him to believe more or display more faith. Elijah just needs to sleep and eat. Twice the angel comes to minister to him, telling him to fill himself with sustenance for the journey.

We might be tempted to over-spiritualise things in our life when things go wrong, telling ourselves that we do not have enough faith or that we have failed God in some way. But we might just need to ask ourselves if we need to stop and take a nap after enjoying a healthy meal. Are we ignoring our bodily needs in our quest to serve God?

Creator God, you have made me in your image and you love me.
Show me how to care for myself in good and healthy ways.

AMY BOUCHER PYE

A gentle whisper

Strengthened by that food, he travelled for forty days and forty nights until he reached Horeb, the mountain of God… And the word of the Lord came to him: 'What are you doing here, Elijah?' He replied, 'I have been very zealous for the Lord God Almighty. The Israelites have rejected your covenant, torn down your altars, and put your prophets to death with the sword. I am the only one left, and now they are trying to kill me too.' The Lord said, 'Go out and stand on the mountain in the presence of the Lord, for the Lord is about to pass by'… But the Lord was not in the wind… the Lord was not in the earthquake… the Lord was not in the fire. And after the fire came a gentle whisper.

Empowered by the food, Elijah journeys to the mountain where Moses had met with God. But he is still feeling grumpy and isolated. Claiming that he is the only one left standing up for God, he lists the sins of God's people: they have not kept his laws, they have torn down the places of worship and they have killed those sharing God's message.

What happens next reinforces the surprising nature of God. Where Elijah probably expects God to manifest himself in the powerful displays of wind, earthquake or fire, he does not. Instead, God shows up in a gentle whisper.

How loving is that! Elijah's senses are probably still on high alert after the great victory and then the descent into despair. Being spent emotionally and physically, he might react to an explosive display of God's power. Instead, God limits himself to a soothing and gentle whisper.

Learning to discern God's gentle nudges takes time and practice. But as we incline our ears and our hearts, we will hear him. As we test out what we believe God is saying, checking it against scripture and perhaps talking with a trusted Christian friend, we will gain in confidence and trust. We, like Elijah, can enter into God's presence.

Gentle God, teach me to hear you,
that I can love you and others better.

AMY BOUCHER PYE

A new plan

When Elijah heard it, he pulled his cloak over his face and went out and stood at the mouth of the cave. Then a voice said to him, 'What are you doing here, Elijah?' He replied, 'I have been very zealous for the Lord God Almighty…' The Lord said to him, 'Go back the way you came, and go to the Desert of Damascus. When you get there, anoint Hazael king over Aram. Also, anoint Jehu son of Nimshi king over Israel, and anoint Elisha son of Shaphat from Abel Meholah to succeed you as prophet. Jehu will put to death any who escape the sword of Hazael, and Elisha will put to death any who escape the sword of Jehu. Yet I reserve seven thousand in Israel – all whose knees have not bowed down to Baal and whose mouths have not kissed him.'

Elijah is stuck. God gives him another chance to show that he has changed his grumbling nature, but he repeats the same answer to God's question of why he is there. He is not wrong with this list of complaints against the Israelites, but he is not, as he claims, the last man standing. God, while giving him some new marching orders, tells him that 7,000 still worship him in Israel. He is hardly the last faithful person.

God's instructions will send him back into the fight against Baal. He has been shirking his duties as a prophet, and the Lord does not relieve him of this mandate. Instead God sends him a team, including naming the prophet who will follow him, Elisha. God recognises Elijah's limitations and provides successors who will take the next steps.

I find this part of the story both encouraging and poignant. Elijah did not manage to fulfil the commission without a big wobble, but God does not sideline him completely. Instead God acknowledges the prophet's limitations and makes a new plan. So too does he, undoubtedly at times, with us.

Sovereign God, I know I have limitations, but I ask that you would use me as you wish to share your life and grace. I want to be a vessel of love for you.

AMY BOUCHER PYE

A new path

So Elijah went from there and found Elisha son of Shaphat. He was ploughing with twelve yoke of oxen, and he himself was driving the twelfth pair. Elijah went up to him and threw his cloak around him. Elisha then left his oxen and ran after Elijah. 'Let me kiss my father and mother goodbye,' he said, 'and then I will come with you.' 'Go back,' Elijah replied. 'What have I done to you?' So Elisha left him and went back. He took his yoke of oxen and slaughtered them. He burned the ploughing equipment to cook the meat and gave it to the people, and they ate. Then he set out to follow Elijah and became his servant.

After journeying hundreds of miles, Elijah finds Elisha, whose name means 'God is my salvation'. The mention of twelve yoke of oxen indicates wealth, as most families would own a single yoke of oxen only. Elijah throwing the coat on him would have signified the office of prophet being conferred on Elisha. The surprised farmer responds by making his plans to leave his way of life.

Notice how well Elisha leaves – he turns his major life change into a party. There will be no going back as he burns his ploughs, but he also invites the community to a knees-up to feast together.

I wonder how Elijah feels as he inducts his successor. His comment, 'What have I done to you?' might seem stand-offish to us, but in the original language it implies that Elisha has the agency to make this decision.

Are we often called to such major life changes? I think of marrying my English husband over two decades ago, with our wedding being the big farewell party. Like Elisha clearing out the farming resources, I sold my car and bits of furniture to move across the Atlantic and start our life together. And although I didn't take on the mantle of a prophet, God had (and has) a place for me here in the UK.

Might God have changes for you to embrace?

Lord of all seasons, help me to embrace the new paths
you may have for me while living in the now.

AMY BOUCHER PYE

The God who sees

'Go down to meet Ahab king of Israel, who rules in Samaria. He is now in Naboth's vineyard, where he has gone to take possession of it. Say to him, "This is what the Lord says: have you not murdered a man and seized his property?" Then say to him, "This is what the Lord says: in the place where dogs licked up Naboth's blood, dogs will lick up your blood – yes, yours!"' Ahab said to Elijah, 'So you have found me, my enemy!' 'I have found you,' he answered, 'because you have sold yourself to do evil in the eyes of the Lord. He says, "I am going to bring disaster on you. I will wipe out your descendants and cut off from Ahab every last male in Israel – slave or free."'

Although Elijah appointed a successor, his work is not yet done. God wants him to announce his judgement over the evil Ahab and Jezebel, who stole a plot of land from Naboth. This landowner refused to sell it because he followed God's laws – he knew it wasn't his to sell – so Jezebel arranged for Naboth to be executed under false charges, allowing Ahab to claim the vineyard. But the royal couple did not realise that God witnessed the act and will put things right.

Elijah's pronouncement might seem extreme – that Ahab and his descendants will be wiped out, scavengers feasting on their bodies. It seems this final crime is the tipping point, the culmination of so much evil that God decides he has had enough. But in a surprising move, Ahab repents in a public display and God relents, putting off the judgement to the next generation.

This story makes me imagine a book with an arresting title, something like 'You Are Your Secrets'. We might think that we can hide our wrongdoing, which might include bitterness, pride, lust or greed, but God sees us in our entirety. He is a merciful God who not only extends forgiveness to us but changes us through the work of the indwelling Holy Spirit. We need not fear his judgement.

Loving and sanctifying God, make me more like Jesus.
Help me show your mercy to others as I share your message
of love and grace.

AMY BOUCHER PYE

One God

'Man of God,' he begged, 'please have respect for my life and the lives of these fifty men, your servants! See, fire has fallen from heaven and consumed the first two captains and all their men. But now have respect for my life!' The angel of the Lord said to Elijah, 'Go down with him; do not be afraid of him.' So Elijah ... told the king, 'This is what the Lord says: is it because there is no God in Israel for you to consult that you have sent messengers to consult Baal-Zebub, the god of Ekron? Because you have done this, you will never leave the bed you are lying on. You will certainly die!' So he died, according to the word of the Lord that Elijah had spoken.

After Ahab's death, his son Ahaziah becomes king and continues his father's evil ways. When he suffers a life-threatening injury, he looks not to the Lord for help but to Baal. Thus God gives Elijah one last mission of judgement.

The king tussles with the man of God, trying to exert his power as he sends three companies of troops, each with 50 men and the captain. After the first two companies die by fire coming out of heaven – clearly the power lies with the man of God – the third captain wisely fears for his life and approaches Elijah humbly. This group of men are spared, but Elijah is not given a message of mercy for the king. He will still die because he consulted the false god.

Elijah therefore continues the theme of God being the only true god. God will brook no rivals and tolerate no synchronicity of blended worship. His word is the final one.

Today God still longs for us to worship him without turning to other gods. We might protest, thinking that gods like Baal live only in history. But other gods fill our minds and hearts today, such as success, power, accomplishments, relationships, ideals, wealth and a whole other host of things. Take some moments to consider where your loyalties lie, asking God to open your eyes that you might serve him only.

Holy God, turn my eyes to you
and help me to love you with all of my heart.

AMY BOUCHER PYE

Succession

Elijah said to Elisha, 'Tell me, what can I do for you before I am taken from you?' 'Let me inherit a double portion of your spirit,' Elisha replied. 'You have asked a difficult thing,' Elijah said, 'yet if you see me when I am taken from you, it will be yours – otherwise, it will not.' As they were walking along and talking together, suddenly a chariot of fire and horses of fire appeared and separated the two of them, and Elijah went up to heaven in a whirlwind. Elisha saw this and cried out, 'My father! My father! The chariots and horsemen of Israel!' And Elisha saw him no more.

Elijah's death is highly unusual, but through it God proclaims that he is the Lord, not Baal. As we come across Elisha's request for a double portion of Elijah's spirit, we might feel he is being greedy, but the meaning of the phrase back then implies the inheritance of the firstborn. Elijah knows that only God can bestow this on Elisha. But he relays how Elisha will know if his request is granted; and it is. The chariot and horses of fire signal God's coming for Elijah and refute Baal's claim to be the 'rider of the clouds'. And Elijah going up to heaven in a whirlwind reveals that Baal is not the storm god; only the true God can claim that title. God wants Elisha and all those gathered to understand that he is the Lord, and that his Spirit will now rest on Elisha.

Elijah did not have an easy commission in his fight against the false gods, but he remained faithful to God even through the ups and downs he experienced. God upheld him in his frailties, ministering to him after his great success and sending him a colleague with whom to share the burden of the position.

I am guessing that you and I may not be called to be prophets, but we have the choice to worship God with purity of heart. Through the help of his Spirit, we can stay focused on God and God alone. May we be those who remain committed to the God of life and light.

Loving God, I want to serve you all my days.
Never leave nor forsake me.

AMY BOUCHER PYE

If you've enjoyed this set of reflections by **Amy Boucher Pye**,
check out her books published with BRF, including...

The Living Cross
*Exploring God's gift
of forgiveness and new life*

9780857465122
£8.99

Celebrating Christmas
Embracing joy through art and reflections

9781800390515
£9.99

To order, visit **brfonline.org.uk** or use the form on page 151.

Living Faith

Revelation 19—22: seeing the light

 I have to admit that I was initially reluctant to write about these chapters of the book of Revelation. My feelings about the book are quite mixed, as I suspect they are for many people. On hearing the name of the book our minds are apt to be filled with images of monstrous dragons, flames, darkness and, of course, those four famous horsemen of the apocalypse.

But this book was not originally written to threaten or frighten, but to encourage and sustain. The Christians to whom this writing was addressed were suffering terribly. Persecuted, tortured, killed, living their lives in constant fear, they longed for words of comfort and support. And it is in these last chapters that we find some of the most beautiful language of loving reassurance that exists. Which of us who have experienced suffering can not be upheld by the promise of a time when there is no more 'mourning or crying or pain' (Revelation 21:4, NIV)? Who is not immeasurably moved by the picture of our Lord God tenderly wiping every tear from our eyes? The picture of the new Jerusalem, with its golden streets and gates kept wide open all day (and there is no night), brings such light and hope into our darkest times, that we can almost see the lamb of God, shining into our pain, bringing healing and love.

Those times have not yet arrived – and yet all has already been accomplished. It is our task while on this earth to hold the flame of hope and faith so high that it lights up not only our lives but the lives of those around us, dispelling the darkness, enabling us to see clearly that the victory lies with God and that death has been defeated.

It seems as if disease and warfare will never fully vanish from the horizon, as we move from Covid to conflict, apprehensive for the future. But I do not despair, because the promises in these chapters are written by one whose words are 'trustworthy and true' (22:6), who holds in his loving, merciful hands the beginning and the end of all times.

'Amen. Come, Lord Jesus. The grace of the Lord Jesus be with God's people. Amen' (22:20–21).

SALLY WELCH

All things new

And from the throne came a voice saying, 'Praise our God, all you his servants and all who fear him, small and great.' Then I heard what seemed to be the voice of a great multitude, like the sound of many waters and like the sound of mighty thunderpeals, crying out, 'Hallelujah! For the Lord God the Almighty reigns. Let us rejoice and exult and give him the glory.'

I have the good fortune to be married to a confirmed optimist, who has a rock-solid belief that things will turn out fine. It is a family joke that he will have written on his gravestone 'Everything's probably going to be alright'. Such is his good humour and unflappable disposition that things usually do turn out alright in the long run, even if the times in between can be challenging.

However, this optimism is not always appropriate – sometimes the thing that we most feared would happen actually does, and I consider it my role in our partnership to provide some steely realism, perhaps even a dose of pessimism, to offset the constant cheerfulness.

But then I challenge myself to avoid sinking into a mindset that consistently anticipates the worst, that never looks on the bright side; I must seek ways of counteracting 'preparing for the worst'. For me the answer was a 'gratitude and praise journal'. Every morning I write down three things I am grateful for, three things for which I thank my creator God and offer him praise. Some days it takes only five minutes – days when I look forward to visits from the family or interesting events at church. On days which contain difficult meetings or challenging situations, it might take slightly longer. But always there will be three things. This discipline sets the mood of the day – I confront my great good fortune, put my troubles in perspective and remind myself that although I don't know what the future holds, I do know who holds the future.

Praise to the Holiest in the height,
and in the depth be praise:
in all his words most wonderful,
most sure in all his ways.
(John Henry Newman, 1801–90)

SALLY WELCH

Dark times

When the thousand years are over, Satan will be released from his prison and will go out to deceive the nations in the four corners of the earth – Gog and Magog – and to gather them for battle. In number they are like the sand on the seashore. They marched across the breadth of the earth and surrounded the camp of God's people, the city he loves.

My study is one of my favourite places. The window looks out on to our garden, with a lawn sloping down to a field and the railway station at the bottom of the hill. The land rises beyond the station, up to the edge of the Wychwood Forest, one of the country's ancient woodlands. Day after day I look out at an ever-changing scene, as the seasons roll on. Today as I write, it is springtime, and the sky is that light blue with white fluffy clouds that so many English pastoral painters try to capture. The daffodils are dancing bravely in the chilly wind, but the promise of warmer days is evident and already the trees are covered in a haze of tiny green leaves. The world seems new, fresh and brimming with life.

We live in 'between times': the old order has passed away and the new one has arrived, but not yet. Our world is still wrapped in the graveclothes of sin and wickedness; destruction and corruption still pollute God's creation. It is easy to despair when we hear the news which seems to be only of darkness and death on all fronts. It is easy to despair when we witness the fear and sadness of so many people in so many places. Hope might seem to have disappeared, becoming merely a memory, a glimpse dimly perceived. Then it may be that we need to leave our homes, our offices, our 'inside' places and look beyond ourselves to the glory of creation that surrounds us. Even a bunch of flowers or a scattering of seeds in a window box can show us the promise of new life and bring us hope once more.

'Our Lord has written the promise of resurrection, not in books alone, but in every leaf in springtime' (Martin Luther, 1483–1546).

SALLY WELCH

The book of the dead

Then I saw a great white throne and him who was seated on it. The earth and the heavens fled from his presence, and there was no place for them. And I saw the dead, great and small, standing before the throne, and books were opened. Another book was opened, which is the book of life. The dead were judged according to what they had done as recorded in the books.

It is Halloween, and shop windows are full of cobwebs and cauldrons, pumpkins and black hats. This evening, young children in carefully escorted groups will knock on the doors of previously alerted households in order to receive spooky sweets and more chocolate than is good for anyone. Later on, groups of young people might well be more adventurous, carrying out acts of mischief under cover of darkness, running off whooping and shouting with delight at their misdoings.

It seems like innocent fun, but many churches now offer an alternative to Halloween activities in the shape of 'light parties' and other events, hoping to draw children and young people away from the attractions of the dark and towards the light and love of Christ. The aim is also to divert attention away from yet another commercial opportunity for companies to draw people into consumerism.

We may have different approaches to the 'safety' or otherwise of tangling, however lightly, with the forces of darkness. But however we feel about the Eve of All Saints, we can use the occasion to look forward to the time when we will live forever in the light, when God dwells with us and we with him, when the 'secrets of the heart' (Psalm 44:21) will be revealed. We may feel completely optimistic about this time, but many of us will feel differently.

So while we enjoy the chocolate cakes with oozy red filling, the plastic fingernails and pointy teeth, we remember that they carry a warning with them too: the time will come when deeds of darkness will be revealed in the light, and we would do well to prepare for that time.

'Again Jesus spoke to them, saying, "I am the light of the world. Whoever follows me will never walk in darkness but will have the light of life"'
(John 8:12, NRSV).

SALLY WELCH

A new earth

Then I saw a new heaven and a new earth; for the first heaven and the first earth had passed away, and the sea was no more. And I saw the holy city, the new Jerusalem, coming down out of heaven from God, prepared as a bride adorned for her husband. And I heard a loud voice from the throne saying, 'See, the home of God is among mortals. He will dwell with them; they will be his peoples, and God himself will be with them and be their God.'

Few people remain unmoved by the intensity of journeying alongside the sick and the dying, sharing the road as they accompany someone they love along those last few steps of their earthly pilgrimage. It can be a wonderful, curiously life-affirming time, or one filled with sorrow and pain. Each death is unique, and every loss of life honoured by God.

After such a time, a passage such as this can bring so much comfort. But it is also suitable for other times, as we reflect on what it means to worship a God who makes all things new (see v. 5). Notice that he does not make 'all new things'; instead the grit and the dirt are cleaned away, the damage and the broken are repaired and made whole, the lost are found and brought home. Notice too that this action is taking place in the present; we look towards a future without death and pain, but we can see right now that the parts of creation which we think are past redemption can be renewed and brought back to their original perfection.

And this is the case not just with things but with people also. As we look with loving eyes on those we find difficult, as we strive to care for the wounded and broken, as we ask for God's help to forgive those whose humanity has been corrupted beyond recognition, we can do so with faith in his promise that all will be made new, that restoration is not just a possibility but a future fact.

Lord, help us to wipe the tears of pain and grief from our eyes
and see where you are working in our world.
And where we see this, help us to join in. Amen

SALLY WELCH

All things new

'He will wipe every tear from their eyes. Death will be no more; mourning and crying and pain will be no more, for the first things have passed away.' And the one who was seated on the throne said, 'See, I am making all things new.' Also he said, 'Write this, for these words are trustworthy and true.' Then he said to me, 'It is done! I am the Alpha and the Omega, the Beginning and the End.'

I have a friend who is an excellent potter. The concentration they maintain is intense: they allow no distractions, only stopping after the artwork has been produced. Occasionally, mistakes are made: rims aren't perfectly spherical, the base is not thin enough, the end result somehow a mismatch with the artist's vision. Then, swiftly, the pot is crushed and it becomes nothing more than a lump of clay once more. Failure instantly forgotten, the artist begins again, once more focused on translating imagination into object, creating something beautiful and unique out of the gifts of the earth.

As with the artist, so with us. We too must create from the raw material of our lives something which reflects the beauty of our creator. The battle between good and evil has already been won, and good has triumphed. It says so here – 'It is done!' (v. 6). The war is over. There remain only the occasional skirmishes, the grubby vestiges of evil, like some vanquished monster whose limbs flail in their death throes. We are already living in victory, and our lives should reflect this.

Let us not agonise over the minor defeats but rejoice in the eternal reign of our God which has already begun. Let us not put all our energies into irrelevant activities but focus on the things that matter. Let us work to reveal the kingdom which has already come, worship the Lord who lives among us and invite others to share in the joy, love and hope which is ours through the incarnation and resurrection of Jesus Christ.

Thine be the glory
Risen conquering Son
Endless is the victory
Thou o'er death hast won.
(Richard Birch Hoyle, 1875–1939)

SALLY WELCH

The water of life

'To the thirsty I will give water without cost from the spring of the water of life. Those who are victorious will inherit all this, and I will be their God and they will be my children'… Jesus answered her, 'If you knew the gift of God and who it is that asks you for a drink, you would have asked him and he would have given you living water.'

The similarity of these two passages is obvious and poignant. In the verse from John's gospel, Jesus is speaking to a Samaritan woman – the one forced to come in the heat of the day to draw water because her nationality and lifestyle had made her an outcast; the one whose opinion of herself had become as low as the opinions others had about her. But she has another identity: she is the one whom Jesus talks with, the one whom he chooses to tell others about him, the one to whom he offers the water of life.

Images of water abound in the hot dry lands of the Bible, for all life depends upon it yet it can be scarce and difficult to find. Its presence is precious, and it is never taken for granted. It should be shared with others, because we too might one day lack water and ask it of another. Yet here it is not only shared but offered abundantly, with generosity, asking nothing in return. If you are thirsty, just ask and it will be given to you.

What a wonderful, glorious, generous God we have, that the gift of eternal life is available to us simply for the asking! And how should we respond to that generosity? By taking God up on it! By accepting the gift that he offers, by drinking deep and then by offering that same gift to others. We should set no conditions, erect no barriers, demand no set behaviour. It is not ours to judge who should receive, who is 'worthy' – ours is simply to offer and to rejoice when another drinks.

I heard the voice of Jesus say,
'Behold, I freely give
the living water, thirsty one;
stoop down and drink and live.'
(Horatius Bonar, 1808–89)

SALLY WELCH

It's all in the detail

And in the spirit he carried me away to a great, high mountain and showed me the holy city Jerusalem coming down out of heaven from God. It has the glory of God and a radiance like a very rare jewel, like jasper, clear as crystal. It has a great, high wall with twelve gates, and at the gates twelve angels, and on the gates are inscribed the names that are the names of the twelve tribes of the Israelites: on the east three gates, on the north three gates, on the south three gates, and on the west three gates… He also measured its wall, one hundred forty-four cubits by human measurement, which the angel was using.

My father is a model railway enthusiast. With diligent use of emotional blackmail he has persuaded me to make the scenery while he concentrates on the electronics. We are working in N Gauge, and the models are really small but incredibly detailed: houses have tiny curtains; shops have displays of tinned goods. These details make it come truly alive; they turn a piece of grey stamped cardboard into something which sparks the imagination and invites one into a miniature world.

One of the glories of this description of the holy city is its attention to detail, and each and every detail means something. The new Jerusalem will have a radiance as clear as crystal; everyone will see God 'face to face'. The high walls of the city symbolise how ordered and controlled it is – safety and shelter lie within. Its twelve gates will always be open (Revelation 21:25) – everyone will be given the chance to enter, and no one will be shut out. The city itself is huge: there is space for everyone, for all time. It is laid out like a square, complete in itself. The treasure with which it is filled will echo the human treasure that will be gathered within – and all will serve to glorify God.

This is surely the ideal for our own earthly communities – places where nobody is ignored or excluded and within whose boundaries all may feel safe.

Lord, help me to see the new Jerusalem
in the imagination of my heart. Amen

SALLY WELCH

Imagine, then imagine some more

The angel who talked with me had a measuring rod of gold to measure the city, its gates and its walls. The city was laid out like a square, as long as it was wide. He measured the city with the rod and found it to be 12,000 stadia in length, and as wide and high as it is long… The wall was made of jasper, and the city of pure gold, as pure as glass. The foundations of the city walls were decorated with every kind of precious stone. The first foundation was jasper, the second sapphire, the third agate, the fourth emerald, the fifth onyx, the sixth ruby, the seventh chrysolite, the eighth beryl, the ninth topaz, the tenth turquoise, the eleventh jacinth, and the twelfth amethyst.

It is hard to believe, but Brighton Pavilion was originally a modest lodging house, rented by George, Prince of Wales, in the 1780s. The small house was rebuilt and extended many times until it reached truly splendid proportions and the glamour and luxury of the interior matched the richness of the outside architecture. Entering the building one cannot help but be overwhelmed by the lavishness of the furniture and furnishings. Setting aside the ethics of Prince George's lifestyle, it is possible simply to gasp in amazement at the sunburst carpet in the music room or the details of the hand-painted Chinese wallpaper.

I am always reminded of Brighton Pavilion when I read this passage. What an amazing picture the writer conjures up. He uses every precious stone, every detail of luxury and richness. Never mind the practicality of gold streets 'transparent as glass', we are just meant to allow our minds to wonder.

During our dark and gloomy times, it is good to let our imaginations simply run riot as we stop and consider what heaven might be like, and this passage helps us do just that. Imagine something as different as possible from your present circumstances, we are being told. 'Imagine a place that glitters with jewels, a place so rich that riches can be put on public display without fear of damage or loss. Imagine something at the far extremes of your imagination, then imagine a little bit further: that's what heaven is like.'

Lord, help me to imagine. Amen

SALLY WELCH

Which temple?

I saw no temple in the city, for its temple is the Lord God the Almighty and the Lamb... The Jews then said to him, 'What sign can you show us for doing this?' Jesus answered them, 'Destroy this temple, and in three days I will raise it up.' The Jews then said, 'This temple has been under construction for forty-six years, and will you raise it up in three days?' But he was speaking of the temple of his body.

I am a passionate believer in the value of church buildings, particularly those in country villages and small towns. They can be the most valuable assets of a community, symbolising a link to a communal past and a legacy for future generations, as well as being precious places for all who need space for reflection and prayer, providing opportunities for thanksgiving and lament, celebration and contemplation. Often physically situated at the centre of a community, they can provide a still point in the midst of change, speaking profoundly and personally to all who enter. They can serve as unifying structures: open to all members of a community. As guardians of this space, church congregations should recognise their responsibility and work hard at maintaining church buildings so that they may continue to serve their purpose long into the future.

However, necessary though a careful, thoughtful, appreciative engagement with church buildings is, we must always be on our guard that we do not cross that dangerous line between caring for a physical structure more than we care for the community it houses and serves. When we are anxious and uncertain about our futures, when we face challenges or setbacks, unexplained disasters or accidents, it is easy to place our hope and trust in what we can see and touch, rather than that which we can only know in our hearts and minds. We must not slip into the idolatry of building-worship, which seeks always to focus our attention on brick and stone rather than the love of God and neighbour which lies at the heart of the Christian faith.

Perhaps this verse in Revelation should be carved over the doorway of every church, as a reminder that our certainty, our security, our hope for the future lies not in the 'temple' of the merely physical, but in almighty God.

Lord, help me to put my trust only in you. Amen

SALLY WELCH

Gates

The city has no need of sun or moon to shine on it, for the glory of God is its light, and its lamp is the Lamb. The nations will walk by its light, and the kings of the earth will bring their glory into it. Its gates will never be shut by day – and there will be no night there. People will bring into it the glory and the honour of the nations.

The visitors' book in a church always makes an interesting read. Sometimes our hearts will be wrung by the requests for prayer that are left in there, poignant appeals for divine aid from the lost and the lonely, the sick and the frightened. Sometimes there will be notes on the occasion that prompted the visit – perhaps a wedding anniversary or a nostalgic trip back to a home church. Some of the most frequent messages will be notes of gratitude to those who care for the building, and in particular, those faithful souls who unlock the doors each morning and lock them again each evening so that those who are seeking sanctuary might find it inside. Again and again, research shows that the single most important thing we do with respect to our church buildings is to open our 'gates' and let people in.

But there exist other gates, barriers which might prevent people from entering our buildings, from engaging with the message of grace which is at the heart of the gospel. They might be self-imposed – things which we as missionaries of the church can do little about, and for which we can carry no responsibility. But we might be unintentional 'gatekeepers' by our words and attitudes, sending messages that visitors are not welcome, that enquirers will not be tolerated, that membership is not open to all but limited to the elite few who know how to 'behave' in church, who say the 'right' words or even simply stand up at the 'right' moments.

We are not the gatekeepers to the kingdom. We do not decide who can enter and who must stay outside the walls of the new Jerusalem. The gates are wide open all the time – let everyone enter!

Lord, help me to keep open the gates of your kingdom. Amen

SALLY WELCH

Soothing the stings

Then the angel showed me the river of the water of life, bright as crystal, flowing from the throne of God and of the Lamb through the middle of the street of the city. On either side of the river is the tree of life with its twelve kinds of fruit, producing its fruit each month, and the leaves of the tree are for the healing of the nations.

My family was a great one for being outdoors. The holidays were mostly spent outside and even in the rainiest, coldest of weather, weekend walks were obligatory. We lived in the country and were free to explore lanes and footpaths, pick blackberries, play in rivers and streams. There were mishaps of course, the most common of which was being stung by nettles. When this happened, everyone joined in the search for dock leaves, whose soothing sap was squeezed on to the affected limb. Apparently there is no science to this, the effect being mostly placebo, but it worked for us!

The leaves of the tree which are for the healing of nations are no placebo: they are the real thing, growing in the new Jerusalem, nourished by the water of life. There are countless numbers of these leaves, an eternal source of healing waiting to be picked and used to soothe the stings suffered by humanity.

Perhaps that is where we come in, the leaf pickers, carrying the gift of healing to those who need it, offering a renewable source of health and wholeness to all who wish. The healing is for all nations; no one is excluded, no one is judged and found unworthy of healing. Our role is not to determine who should be 'healed', because we follow a wildly generous, outrageously merciful God, who forgives all who ask, who opens the door to all who knock. Our role is to offer, open-handed, all that we can to help the wounded around us.

Lord, we pray for the healing of the nations; show us how we can share your work and bring to life the vision of your kingdom. Amen

SALLY WELCH

Light

Nothing accursed will be found there any more. But the throne of God and of the Lamb will be in it, and his servants will worship him; they will see his face, and his name will be on their foreheads. And there will be no more night; they need no light of lamp or sun, for the Lord God will be their light, and they will reign forever and ever.

One of my favourite illustrations for talks at a service of baptism involves 'invisible' writing. I show the congregation a special felt-tip pen and demonstrate the fact that it leaves no mark when it is used by drawing a cross on the palm of my hand. I then shine an ultraviolet light on my hand which shows up the cross in purple. I speak about how pens and stamps like this are sometimes used to show that people have paid the entrance fee for amusement parks or nightclubs. Invisible to the naked eye, it shows up boldly when the light is shone on it.

So too with the cross that is made upon the forehead of the baptism candidate. Marked using the oil of baptism, freshly blessed each Maundy Thursday at cathedral chrism services, this cross leaves no visible sign after the oil has dried. Yet a cross has been made on each person's soul, and in the light of the end times, the cross will shine brightly, marking out individuals whose lives have been bought by the saving act of redemption made once for all people by Jesus Christ.

But that is in the future: how do those of us whose souls have been engraved with the sign of cross live in the in-between times? I think we strive to live as if that cross marked on our forehead at our baptism is still boldly shining, revealing to the world that how we speak and act must be seen through the lens of our belief in a merciful God, whose love bathes each of us in a radiant light.

Lord, let the light of your love shine through me. Amen

SALLY WELCH

'Come'

The angel said to me, 'These words are trustworthy and true. The Lord, the God who inspires the prophets, sent his angel to show his servants the things that must soon take place'… 'I, Jesus, have sent my angel to give you this testimony for the churches. I am the Root and the Offspring of David, and the bright Morning Star.' The Spirit and the bride say, 'Come!' And let the one who hears say, 'Come!' Let the one who is thirsty come; and let the one who wishes take the free gift of the water of life.

It is my good fortune to be involved with a 'stay and play' group for under-fives and their parents and carers. We meet once a week and spend an hour and a half playing with toys, singing songs and eating healthy snacks, as well as the occasional biscuit. The adults can enjoy each other's company, while the children learn how to share toys and why it is not a good idea to hit another child.

It is interesting to watch the children as they enter the room. Some are bold and confident, happy to pitch straight in to the serious work of play. Others hesitate on the threshold, needing time to adjust to the new setting. Then a friend of theirs might notice their arrival and run up joyfully to greet them, or one of the helpers will encourage them gently by pointing out the different activities they could engage with. Soon even the shyest will join in, and the time flies by.

We all approach Jesus' invitation to a new life in our own unique way. Some of us need no encouragement; others might need time to explore such a radically different way of existing, with its values and priorities so at odds with much of society. We must remember our own journeys of faith as we accompany others on their journey, offering gentle non-judgemental encouragement, respecting their pace and rejoicing in each step, however hesitant, towards the 'bright morning star' of all our lives.

I looked to Jesus, and I found
in him my star, my sun;
and in that light of life I'll walk
till travelling days are done.
(Horatius Bonar, 1808–89)

SALLY WELCH

All the saints

I warn everyone who hears the words of the prophecy of this scroll: if anyone adds anything to them, God will add to that person the plagues described in this scroll... He who testifies to these things says, 'Yes, I am coming soon.' Amen. Come, Lord Jesus. The grace of the Lord Jesus be with God's people. Amen.

During my time in the church, I have grown to appreciate our saints and the extraordinary variety of gifts and skills they brought to the church. St Hugh of Lincoln was an awesome administrator, who brought order to a troubled abbey. Then there is St Ambrose, about whom it is said that as an infant, a swarm of bees settled on his face while he lay in his cradle, leaving behind a drop of honey. This was considered a sign of his future eloquence and honeyed tongue and in due course he became bishop of Milan. St Brigid was the abbess of a great convent and was to convert the king of a hostile tribe with a cross of rushes from the floor. So it continues – there are many wonderful stories of some amazingly godly and gifted people.

Interestingly, apart from the obligatory miracles, these saints do not have a lot in common with each other – high class, low class, learned, ordinary. They do, however, share a profound love for God and deep desire to know him better. It is their love for God from which everything else flows and towards which all gifts and skills are channelled. This is the amazing, wonderful thing that unites them.

One of the glories – and challenges – of church communities is that they draw together all sorts of people who might not have a great deal in common. However, we are also united by our desire to serve and love God and neighbour, to carry out God's work on earth by making 'all things new' (Revelation 21:5, ESV) – bringing hope where there is none, showing love to the unloved and rejoicing in God's creation.

Oh, blest communion, fellowship divine!
We feebly struggle, they in glory shine;
yet all are one in thee, for all are thine.
(William Walsham How, 1823–97)

SALLY WELCH

Romans 1—6

Romans is the only book written by Paul to a church with whom he had no previous relationship. There were Jews from Rome present on the Day of Pentecost (Acts 2:10) and therein may be the origin of the church. Paul's letter to Romans is different to his other New Testament letters, which focus more on the church with its challenges and problems. Romans focuses on God and his plan for the salvation of the world. The word 'God' occurs 153 times in the letter, compared with 'law' (78), 'Christ' (65), 'sin' (48), 'Lord' (43) and 'faith' (40). Romans deals with a few different themes but, as much as it can be, it is a book about God.

When Paul wrote Romans around AD58 he had been a Christian for 20 years and was ready for his definitive telling of the Christian salvation story that joined the dots between his time before and his time after his vision of Christ on the road to Damascus (Acts 9:1–9). Paul's crowning achievement is to distil his Jewish heritage and his Christian vision into one central idea: the believer is made right with God (justified) through faith in Christ.

The genius of Romans is that it sums up the effect of Jesus' crucifixion and resurrection in just three words: 'justification by faith'. To establish this as the heart of God's relationship in Christ with the world, there are three things that Paul needs to answer. Is this a message for whole world? (Yes!) Placed alongside the requirements of the law, is this an easy option? (No!) Is this different to how God has acted in the past? (No!)

Paul thought strategically: because of its location, the church in Rome had a special visibility and opportunity to reach throughout the empire. The letter is a manifesto of the faith written for the city at the centre of the known world; Rome would be a baseline of communication across the known world.

The ultimate strategist in God's plan of salvation is the Holy Spirit: Acts 19:21 describes Paul's determination to visit Rome. Ironically when he did get to Rome, it was as a shipwrecked prisoner. It may be that you will get what you pray for but not in the way that you expect.

BOB MAYO

Paul introduces himself

Paul, a servant of Christ Jesus, called to be an apostle and set apart for the gospel of God… through him we received grace and apostleship to call all the Gentiles to the obedience that comes from faith for his name's sake… To all in Rome who are loved by God and called to be his holy people: Grace and peace to you from God our Father and from the Lord Jesus Christ.

Paul introduces himself with what Martin Luther described as 'modesty' and 'majesty'. He describes himself as an apostle and a servant. An apostle speaks with the authority of the one who sent him; the servant is the lowest of the low. The role of an apostle is majestic: preaching the gospel, teaching the church, baptising and other pastoral duties. Paul's role as a private individual is modest. He describes himself as a servant of Christ Jesus. It is the same description used by Moses (Joshua 1:2), Joshua (Joshua 24:29), Amos (Amos 3:7) and Jeremiah (Jeremiah 7:25), all of whom described themselves as God's servants.

God's calling on Paul's life was not for a special honour, but for a special responsibility. He was to be an apostle with a responsibility to call the Gentiles to the obedience that comes from faith for his name's sake (v. 5); 'obedience through faith' is the original phrase for the hymn: 'Trust and obey, trust and obey, there is no other way to be happy in Jesus than to trust and obey.'

Paul's submission to God gives an example of someone ready to exercise his position in society for the good of others. His first words after his conversion were, 'Lord, what do you want me to do'; he was ready to do unpleasant work (1 Corinthians 4:12); he was ready to preach and serve (Romans 1:15); he was ready to suffer (Acts 21:13); he was ready to die for his faith (2 Timothy 4:6).

God may give you a specific task for a time, or people to take care of for a period. God's calling on your life will be shaped by the circumstances in which you live, the type of person you are and the people that you live among. Everyone has a calling, and it always involves people.

BOB MAYO

Three times of salvation

I am not ashamed of the gospel, because it is the power of God that brings salvation to everyone who believes: first to the Jew, then to the Gentile. For in the gospel the righteousness of God is revealed – a righteousness that is by faith from first to last, just as it is written: 'The righteous will live by faith.'

This passage contains within it the central theme of Romans and the heart of the Christian gospel: we are declared righteous (or we might say 'justified') in God through faith in Christ. The word 'righteousness', appears over 35 times in Romans. Sometimes the word is translated 'righteousness'; other times, 'justification'. In Romans, faith means a total acceptance and an absolute trust. Our acceptance of God and God's choice of us meet in faith; it is as if we open a door and find that God is waiting for us there already.

God brings salvation to all who believe. There are three times of salvation: past, present and future. Christ has paid the penalty of sin through his death on the cross (past). The Holy Spirit fights the power of sin, as we commit our lives to Christ (present). Christ will overcome the presence of sin at his second coming to earth (future).

In the Bible, 'salvation' refers to both physical and spiritual wholeness; there is not the same distinction in our modern thinking, where we conceive of salvation as entirely spiritual. In the Bible we find instances of (physical) salvation from illness (Matthew 9:21). We also find references to (spiritual) salvation from sin (Matthew 1:21).

When Paul says that he was not 'ashamed', he meant that the confidence he had in the gospel was not misplaced. He was explaining to the Romans that, despite spending time in prison because of his faith, he did not believe that he was wrong to identify with Jesus and to make proclaiming Jesus' message his life's work.

It is easy to feel awkward or embarrassed when talking about our faith.
In a sophisticated city like Rome, it might have been easy
to be embarrassed by a God centred on a crucified saviour
and embraced by the lowest class of people.

BOB MAYO

God's truth is clear for all to see

**The wrath of God is being revealed from heaven against all the godless-
ness and wickedness of people, who suppress the truth by their wickedness, since what may be known about God is plain to them, because
God has made it plain to them. For since the creation of the world God's
invisible qualities – his eternal power and divine nature – have been
clearly seen, being understood from what has been made, so that people
are without excuse.**

God has given a general revelation that is clear both in creation and in
the hearts and minds of human beings. The issue is not that they did not
know God; the issue is that they *did* know God but did nothing about it.
Ignorance is no defence.

This means, according to the Christian faith, that judgement is part of the
natural order. Actions have consequences: deliberate, conscious and wilful
sin arouses God's wrath. There is in the world a natural order: break the laws
of agriculture, and the harvest fails; break the laws of health, and your body
suffers; deliberately break the laws of God, and his wrath will be revealed.

Without the salvation that Jesus Christ brings, one could only stand
condemned, subject to God's holy wrath. Paul's goal is not just to proclaim
the good news of salvation, but also to demonstrate its absolute necessity.
As far as Paul is concerned, unless there is something to be saved from there
is no reason to be talking about salvation.

Paul speaks of God's wrath, not human anger. The difference between the
two is that, whereas human anger can often be random and inconsistent,
there is nothing unpredictable or uncontrolled about God's holy wrath; it
is the just and ordered response of his holiness towards evil.

God's love saved us from his holy wrath through the gift of his own dear
Son, who bore our sins and took our punishment on himself. As John Stott
(1921–2011) says: 'God himself gave himself to save us from himself.'

---

*The idea that God reveals himself through the creation brings a particular
urgency to the debate about how to care for the environment:
we are left without excuse for not being aware of the issues at hand.*

BOB MAYO

Judgement

At whatever point you judge another, you are condemning yourself, because you who pass judgment do the same things. Now we know that God's judgment against those who do such things is based on truth. So when you, a mere human being, pass judgment on them and yet do the same things, do you think you will escape God's judgment? Or do you show contempt for the riches of his kindness, forbearance and patience, not realising that God's kindness is intended to lead you to repentance?

There are consequences to our being justified by faith, one of which is our acceptance that the judging of people is God's responsibility and not ours. We are to make judgements, in the sense of discernment, wisdom or evaluation: 'the person with the Spirit makes judgements about all things' (1 Corinthians 2:15). However, we are not to 'judge' others in the sense of condemning them – condemnation kills hope in people, causes them to feel shame and creates division.

For us to judge another person shows pride – how do we know what someone is thinking? Only God knows what is in a person's heart. To condemn another person repeats the sin of Adam, because it is us putting our selfish selves in the place of God – who are we to judge our neighbour (James 4:12)?

God is patient and forbearing because his justice has already been served through the death of Christ. Our sins have been paid for, in advance, and so he can wait for us to repent.

God is patient and forbearing because he is kind. 'Kindness' is not how we intuitively think of God. The word translated 'kind' in this passage is the same word translated as 'easy' when Jesus says: 'Take my yoke [of kindness] upon you and learn from me, for I am gentle and humble in heart, and you will find rest for your souls. For my yoke is easy and my burden is light' (Matthew 11:29–30).

Judgement can set people free as easily as hold them captive. Judgement, in and of itself, is a neutral term; a person can be judged and found guilty or innocent. It is our wonderfully kind, tolerant and patient God who judges us.

BOB MAYO

Equality

All who sin apart from the law will also perish apart from the law, and all who sin under the law will be judged by the law. For it is not those who hear the law who are righteous in God's sight, but it is those who obey the law who will be declared righteous. (Indeed, when Gentiles, who do not have the law, do by nature things required by the law, they are a law for themselves, even though they do not have the law.)

Justification by faith in Christ means that all are equal in God's eyes; salvation cannot be earned, and no one person is considered any more deserving of merit than another. The religious leaders of the time had no inbuilt advantage over others, just because they were the children of Abraham and the people of the law: 'Do not think you can say to yourselves', said John the Baptist, '"We have Abraham as our father." I tell you that out of these stones God can raise up children for Abraham' (Matthew 3:9).

Justification by faith means equality: rich and poor stand equal before God. It was no longer the case that obedience to what was required by the law made someone righteous; rather that righteousness through faith expressed itself naturally through obedience to what was required by the law.

'Righteous' is a term from the law courts. It denotes the status someone has when the court has found in their favour. William Barclay (1907–78) described the effect of righteousness as 'God treating the sinner as if he had not been a sinner at all; thus, to be justified by God is to start a new relationship based on love, confidence and friendship, instead of one based on distance, enmity and fear.' This is the beating heart of the gospel which is spelt out within the pages of Romans.

Christianity is a shared faith. Church is not an optional extra; it is where our belief comes to life, and we collectively live out our righteousness through faith. A church is a community whose foundation is a shared faith in Jesus Christ. All are to be made welcome.

'There is neither Jew nor Gentile, neither slave nor free,
nor is there male and female, for you are all one in Christ Jesus'
(Galatians 3:28).

BOB MAYO

Do we still need the law?

Now we know that whatever the law says, it says to those who are under the law, so that every mouth may be silenced and the whole world held accountable to God. Therefore no one will be declared righteous in God's sight by the works of the law; rather, through the law we become conscious of our sin.

Justification through faith is a simple message but not an easy option; it does not undo anything of what God has done previously through the law. In any context in which a person operates, law acts as a framework to help them to realise when and whether they have done something wrong: the driver only realises that he is going the wrong way when he sees a traffic sign; the sportsman only accepts that he has committed a foul when the referee blows his whistle. Similarly, the Christian believer only understands that he has sinned through his knowledge of the law.

Once conscious of our sin, we are aware of our need for forgiveness. The law is our tutor to lead us to Christ (Galatians 3:24); it helps us to realise our need of God's grace. Martin Luther said that the law was given in order that we might seek after grace; grace was given in order that we might fulfil the law.

Jesus said, 'Do not think that I have come to abolish the Law or the Prophets; I have not come to abolish them but to fulfil them' (Matthew 5:17). Fulfilling the law is different to keeping the law. Keeping the law is a question of obedience and morality; one can keep the law resentfully. Fulfilling the law is a question of faith, love and trust in God and is a work of the Holy Spirit. Our role is to have faith; we are made righteous through our faith. This brings right relationships with others and a right relationship with God.

We are made right with God through divine mercy rather than human merit. The prodigal son thought that he could earn his father's approval by taking on a position as a hired servant (Luke 15:19). Instead, he had simply to be ready to receive his father's love.

BOB MAYO

A universal message?

This righteousness is given through faith in Jesus Christ to all who believe. There is no difference between Jew and Gentile, for all have sinned and fall short of the glory of God, and all are justified freely by his grace through the redemption that came by Christ Jesus. God presented Christ as a sacrifice of atonement, through the shedding of his blood – to be received by faith.

Paul wants to demonstrate that God's plan of salvation is for all; it is for the whole world and not simply for God's people. No one is left out or left behind. 'God presented Christ as a sacrifice of atonement' (reconciliation between sinful humankind and the holy God; v. 25). We are freely justified by God's grace because we were guilty of sin and our lives are redeemed through Christ because we were held captive by sin (v. 24).

These verses contain within them a full summary of the gospel. Before we can put our faith in Christ, we must accept that we are sinners in need of salvation and believe the power of Christ's death and resurrection to heal and save us. At the heart of being justified by faith is the recognition that we all 'have sinned and fall short of the glory of God' (v. 23). There are no limits to God's grace: where sin increased, grace increased even more (Romans 5:20). We cannot out-sin the grace of God.

Justification requires our faith to be more than a tacit consent; it requires us to put heart, mind and soul into our belief. As John wrote to the church in Laodicea, be hot or cold, but never lukewarm (Revelations 3:15). Luther said that faith is a living, daring confidence in God's grace. It puts the old Adam to death and makes us altogether different persons in heart and spirit and mind and powers. And it brings the Holy Spirit; it changes us and makes us to be born anew of God (John 3:3).

Faith is not a simple feeling that will alter from circumstance to circumstance; it is a gift from God. Faith is therefore something for which we can pray when we are feeling sad or downcast.

'I do believe; help me overcome my unbelief!',
prayed the man whose son Jesus healed (Mark 9:24).

BOB MAYO

Is justification new?

Against all hope, Abraham in hope believed and so became the father of many nations, just as it had been said to him, 'So shall your offspring be.' Without weakening in his faith, he faced the fact that his body was as good as dead – since he was about a hundred years old – and that Sarah's womb was also dead. Yet he did not waver through unbelief regarding the promise of God, but was strengthened in his faith and gave glory to God, being fully persuaded that God had power to do what he had promised. This is why 'it was credited to him as righteousness.'

If 'Jesus Christ is the same yesterday and today and forever' (Hebrews 13:8), Paul needs to demonstrate that justification by faith is an idea integrated into God's revelation throughout scripture. Paul must demonstrate that it is a whole-Bible doctrine, and not one that first appears here. What Paul does is to show that the life of Abraham, the founding father of Israel, was justified by faith in his time, in the same way that ours is now.

Paul argues that it was Abraham's faith (Hebrews 11:8) not the fact that he had performed the demands of the law that put him into a special relationship with God. Abraham trusted God when he was called to leave his country and go into a strange land (Genesis 12—13); he trusted God when told to sacrifice his son Isaac (Genesis 22:1–2). Abraham was credited as righteous because of his faith (Genesis 15:6).

Our challenges will be different to those faced by Abraham, but our call to faith is the same. What we have in our walk of faith, which was never available to Abraham, is God's revelation through his son Jesus; faith is belief in the truth of the gospel as well as trust in the God of the gospel.

By drawing on the example of Abraham's faith, Paul is looking back to see forward; he is drawing on the stories of the past to learn lessons for the future. The wisdom of those who are older than us or of those who have died can provide helpful insights and ideas for the future.

BOB MAYO

Benefits of being justified

Therefore, since we have been justified through faith, we have peace with God through our Lord Jesus Christ, through whom we have gained access by faith into this grace in which we now stand. And we boast in the hope of the glory of God. Not only so, but we also glory in our sufferings, because we know that suffering produces perseverance; perseverance, character; and character, hope. And hope does not put us to shame, because God's love has been poured out into our hearts through the Holy Spirit, who has been given to us.

The first benefit of justification through faith is that we have peace with God. The peace that Jesus promises is not an absence of conflict: 'Do not suppose that I have come to bring peace to the earth. I did not come to bring peace, but a sword' (Matthew 10:34). Rather, the peace that Jesus promises is a loving confidence: 'I have told you these things, so that in me you may have peace. In this world you will have trouble. But take heart! I have overcome the world' (John 16:33).

The second benefit of justification through faith is that we have full access to God's grace for both our salvation and for our ongoing sanctification. Grace is both God's gift of love as well as his power for our lives. We are sustained by God's grace for our walk in the Lord.

The third benefit of justification through faith is that we can glory in our suffering and hope will not put us to shame because 'God's love has been poured out into our hearts through the Holy Spirit' (v. 5). This passage is Paul's first mention in Romans of both the 'Holy Spirit' and the 'love of God'. We may have expected suffering to be evidence of God's displeasure; the fact that they are bracketed together in a passage about suffering suggests that Paul sees suffering as often being evidence of God's love and not of God's wrath.

Suffering can be transformative. Two people can meet the same situation; it can drive one of them to despair, and in another it can create a sense of hope.

BOB MAYO

Christ died for us

You see, at just the right time, when we were still powerless, Christ died for the ungodly. Very rarely will anyone die for a righteous person, though for a good person someone might possibly dare to die. But God demonstrates his own love for us in this: while we were still sinners, Christ died for us. Since we have now been justified by his blood, how much more shall we be saved from God's wrath through him!

Paul marvels at Jesus' faithfulness in dying for the 'ungodly'. For all the panoramic sweep of his writing, he is at heart a simple believer seeking to be faithful to the faithfulness of his Lord. Paul wrote on another occasion: 'Here is a trustworthy saying that deserves full acceptance: Christ Jesus came into the world to save sinners – of whom I am the worst' (1 Timothy 1:15).

Paul highlights the fact that Christ died for the 'ungodly' because him doing so contains within it an important principle of God's love. We are told to forgive one another, 'just as in Christ God forgave you' (Ephesians 4:32). God's forgiveness is not earned; it is given freely. The unrepentant may not realise that forgiveness is available to them but that does not prevent it being offered by God and by implication so also by us.

Paul never lost his acute awareness of God's grace and of the change that it had made to his life. He received three visions of Jesus that drove his ministry forward: on the road to Damascus (Acts 9:4); in the temple at Jerusalem (Acts 22:17–21); and once while in prison, which led to his decision to head to Rome (Acts 23:11).

The language in Romans is sometimes poetic, with words and ideas repeated to emphasise their importance. Today's passage is one such example: we are made right with God (justified) through his blood (his death for our sin on the cross). Being made right with God, we need never experience his wrath.

Paul was writing a letter that would go on to become a cornerstone of the New Testament, but there is no evidence of self-importance in how he wrote. He was able to hold on to the simplicity of a new life in Christ and never lost the joy of his salvation.

BOB MAYO

Original sin

Therefore, just as sin entered the world through one man, and death through sin, and in this way, death came to all people, because all sinned… But the gift is not like the trespass. For if the many died by the trespass of the one man, how much more did God's grace and the gift that came by the grace of the one man, Jesus Christ, overflow to the many!

The sin of Adam opened us up to original sin; the death of Christ opened us up to the possibility of eternal life. How much harm can one person do and how much good another? Adam and Eve were given one specific law by God, which they disobeyed. The first human sin involved the choice of self-interest over God's authority. The idea that we have an instinct towards sinful conduct is echoed in the Psalms: 'I was sinful at birth, sinful from the time my mother conceived me' (Psalm 51:5).

Paul acknowledges the ongoing hold of 'original' sin on his life: 'What a wretched man I am! Who will rescue me from this body that is subject to death?' (Romans 7:24). Given the ongoing hold of sin, justification is not merely a one-off event, but also a daily occurrence when we realise our need for forgiveness and, once again, put our faith in Christ.

As well as being an individual reality, the sin of Adam, over the generations, has become baked into the ways of the world. Although we may not be directly responsible for them, we still suffer the consequences of these sins of humanity. Structural inequality, corporate greed, war, violence and injustice are core parts of the world which Christ came to save.

The reality of sin means there is a responsibility on our behalf to respond; injustice cannot be left unchallenged. Paul talks about the privilege and the responsibility of being a Christian. Our privilege is that we are justified through God's grace by our faith in Christ. We have multiple responsibilities: to creation (Romans 8:19); to our families (1 Timothy 5:8); and to those more vulnerable than ourselves (Romans 14:1).

Repentance focuses on our actions and what can be done differently; sorrow focuses on ourselves and what we feel about a situation. We are called to repent of our sins, not simply to feel sorry for what we have done.

BOB MAYO

An easy option?

Shall we go on sinning, so that grace may increase? By no means! We are those who have died to sin; how can we live in it any longer? Or don't you know that all of us who were baptised into Christ Jesus were baptised into his death? We were therefore buried with him through baptism into death in order that, just as Christ was raised from the dead through the glory of the Father, we too may live a new life.

Romans reads lyrically at times, and here the same question is asked in three different ways. Between justification and glorification lies sanctification and the Christian's behaviour is the object of Paul's concern. Paul poses the question rhetorically: if an increase in our sinning triggers an increase in God's forgiving, then should the doing of good works not be left optional? (No.)

He asks it as a question of discipleship: what lives are we expected to lead with the sin of Adam pulling us one way and grace and forgiveness through Jesus Christ (Romans 5:15) pulling us the other?

He asks it as a moral question: if we died to sin (in the past), how then can we live in it (in the future)? He is not referring to the literal impossibility of sin. The effect of original sin remains in us throughout our lives: 'for the flesh desires what is contrary to the Spirit, and the Spirit what is contrary to the flesh' (Galatians 5:17). Paul is highlighting the inconsistency of deliberate, conscious wilful sin in the life of a believer.

Paul's answer is to map our lives as believers on to the life of Christ. The death and resurrection of Jesus Christ are not only historical facts but also personal experiences in the life of the believer; knowledge is of no use if it does not lead into practice. We have died to sin to be united with Christ in his resurrection.

Paul says that something life-changing happens in the believer's life. We have a real (although spiritual) death and resurrection with Jesus Christ. We cannot die to sin and rise again with Christ without it changing our life. How has this been so for you?

Paul says that faith in Christ is life-changing: you cannot die to sin and rise again, with Christ, without it transforming your life. What difference does being a Christian make to your life?

BOB MAYO

Dying and living

Now if we died with Christ, we believe that we will also live with him. For we know that since Christ was raised from the dead, he cannot die again; death no longer has mastery over him. The death he died, he died to sin once for all; but the life he lives, he lives to God. In the same way, count yourselves dead to sin but alive to God in Christ Jesus.

Paul is offering a new mindset to the Romans, showing them how to think about their new life in Christ. They are free from sin ('dead to sin') and living for God ('alive to God in Christ'). People are no longer locked into sin because, since Christ has broken the power of sin and death, they can make the decision to live righteously – 'The righteous will live by faith' (Romans 1:17). They have always had the power to choose how to live; now they can choose the power of God in Christ.

Herein is the invitation given to all believers: to have our lives caught up with the life of Christ – 'He who raised Christ from the dead will also give life to your mortal bodies because of his Spirit who lives in you' (Romans 8:11). We are bound by mortality yet also caught up in eternity through Jesus Christ.

The power of the gospel is God; the purpose of the gospel is salvation; the content of the gospel is righteousness through faith; the availability of the gospel is to all. The gospel is not based on a moral system; it is based on a person, Jesus Christ. The evidence of Jesus' humanity is his human birth; the evidence of his deity is his resurrection from the dead. The gospel is not information or advice; it is the power of salvation. It is not philosophy; it is life-changing good news.

The Bible is like a jigsaw puzzle where all the pieces fit together: the Spirit lives in us, as a great treasure in fragile clay jars 'to show that this all-surpassing power is from God and not from us' (2 Corinthians 4:7) – we get things wrong, but to God be the glory in all things!

To be 'dead to sin but alive to God in Christ Jesus', might happen in a single faith-filled moment of rebirth (John 3:3), but it can equally be a promise into which we grow through prayerful, loving, obedient Christian living. Genuine faith is demonstrated by obedient action.

BOB MAYO

Eternal life

When you were slaves to sin, you were free from the control of righteousness. What benefit did you reap at that time from the things you are now ashamed of? Those things result in death! But now that you have been set free from sin and have become slaves of God, the benefit you reap leads to holiness, and the result is eternal life. For the wages of sin is death, but the gift of God is eternal life in Christ Jesus our Lord.

Paul did not write his letter to the church in Rome sitting at a desk alone. The custom at the time would have been for an author to dictate to a scribe who would write out the dictation and work with the author to create the final form of the document. (The name of Paul's scribe was Tertius – see Romans 16:22.)

Two people working together on a text would make for a more dramatic, dialogical style than might be the case for a book written by a single author sitting at a desk and thinking out every word. Here Paul appeals directly to his readers and hearers, asking them to remember what it had been like for them before: it had been, he says, a form of living death.

The Bible refers to spiritual and physical death. One day Jesus invited a man to follow him and become a disciple, but the man refused. He said he would follow Jesus later, but first he wanted to go and bury his father. Jesus responded, 'Follow me, and let the [spiritually] dead bury their own [physically] dead' (Matthew 8:22).

Eternal life, sharing in the knowledge and love of God, cannot be calculated chronologically, as an endless succession of days. The idea of 'eternity' functions outside of and beyond time, but begins the moment we express faith in Christ. John says, 'Whoever believes in the Son has eternal life' (John 3:36).

---

*Following Christ is a daily commitment and not a single one-off decision.
Each day requires a decision for Christ: do you want the 'wages' (of sin)
that are deserved or God's 'gift' of eternal life (in Christ Jesus),
which is freely given.*

BOB MAYO

Mark 1—6: gospel beginnings

All the gospel writers have an individual style. Writing with particular audiences in mind, their emphases are different. They are selective in the material they include. They need to be, for as John explains in his gospel: 'There are also many other things that Jesus did; if every one of them were written down, I suppose that the world itself could not contain the books that would be written' (John 21:25, NRSV).

At first glance, two of the most striking things about Mark's gospel are its brevity and its energetic pace. Jesus and his followers are always on the move. The word translated 'immediately' occurs more than 40 times. Many verses begin with the word 'and'. All this conveys the sense of a collection of incidents rather than an ordered chronicle of how events unfolded.

However, despite the concision and brisk tempo of his account, Mark describes some incidents in greater detail than Matthew, Luke or John. Mark gives names to some people whom the other gospel writers only describe, and he adds some surprising specifics omitted by the other evangelists. For example, in the healing of the blind beggar outside Jericho, only Mark gives us his name – Bartimaeus – and tells us that, as he responded to Jesus' invitation in the chaotic, crowded street, he cast aside his cloak (see Mark 10:46–52; cf. Matthew 20:29–34; Luke 18:35–43). These kinds of details add depth and meaning; they reward careful consideration.

While the authors of some biblical literature are praised for their literary prowess, it seems likely that Mark created his gospel for 'hearers' rather than 'readers'. As you engage with these words on the page, allow them to paint a picture. Let your Spirit-inspired imagination evoke the sounds and smells and atmosphere as Jesus moves from place to place, encounters a host of characters and leaves no life unchanged.

Notice how his authority is gradually revealed as he confronts his critics and demonstrates his influence over nature, illness and spiritual powers. Observe how he refuses to be constrained by the cultural norms or religious rules of his day, and pray for the wisdom and courage to do likewise. See the way he inspires, encourages, rebukes and shapes his followers, and allow him to do the same for you.

STEVE AISTHORPE

My beloved child

The beginning of the good news of Jesus Christ… In those days Jesus came from Nazareth of Galilee and was baptised by John in the Jordan. And just as he was coming up out of the water, he saw the heavens torn apart and the Spirit descending like a dove on him. And a voice came from the heavens, 'You are my Son, the Beloved; with you I am well pleased.'

In 2018 there was much excitement among scholars when a portion of a very ancient document known as Papyrus 137 was made public. Carefully inscribed on the fragile fragment were verses from the opening of the most influential book in the world. Discovering this earliest known piece of what we often call the 'gospel of Mark' will have been a highlight in the lives of some of the people involved. However, Mark's opening words remind us that we have even more cause for rejoicing and eager anticipation as we actually read this book, because this is not actually the 'gospel of Mark'. As proclaimed in the opening sentence, this is the 'gospel (or good news) of Jesus'.

This is not just an ancient and historic document; it is an announcement of the greatest ever news. Jesus was a common name in the first century, but readers are told to make no mistake: this Jesus is 'the Christ', the anointed one, the long-promised saviour and king.

After explaining how John the Baptist prepared the way, fulfilling the prophecy of Isaiah several centuries earlier, Mark takes us to the baptism of Jesus and we hear the affirming words of his (our) Father. In the words of the most quoted Psalm in the New Testament (Psalm 2), Jesus is reminded and assured, 'You are my dearly loved child.' He is given a glimpse of another realm and sees a manifestation of the Spirit, and as we read Mark's account we receive a vision of all three aspects of the Trinity, the three-in-one God in action.

It was before the ministry of Jesus got started that he heard the assurance 'You are my beloved.' Likewise, we are chosen and loved, not because of anything we have done, and sometimes despite it.

'We love because he first loved us' (1 John 4:19).

STEVE AISTHORPE

Follow me

As Jesus passed along the Sea of Galilee, he saw Simon and his brother Andrew casting a net into the sea, for they were fishers. And Jesus said to them, 'Follow me, and I will make you fishers of people.' And immediately they left their nets and followed him. As he went a little farther, he saw James son of Zebedee and his brother John, who were in their boat mending the nets. Immediately he called them, and they left their father Zebedee in the boat with the hired men and followed him.

I wonder whether these two pairs of brothers were friends or rivals. What we know for sure is that having said 'yes' to Jesus, they were thrown together into the most intimate and challenging community imaginable. I wonder what they woke up thinking the next morning and in the weeks and months that followed. Did their response continue to be as wholehearted as their walking away from familiarity and security 'immediately' suggests?

We know otherwise: Simon (later called Peter), despite his unhesitating and unequivocal response on the shores of the Sea of Galilee, would betray Jesus. That call to follow would need to be reissued. When Jesus later says 'Follow me' as part of their post-resurrection conversation (John 21:19), the words would be the same, but Peter's understanding will have changed. He would come to be full of regret for his betrayal, being aware then that the one inviting him was 'the Messiah, the Son of the living God' (Matthew 16:16). The invitation of Jesus is always in a particular context; he invites us from where we are. The focus is always the same ('follow me'), but the implications differ and deepen as the journey progresses and the relationship develops.

One of the most incredible truths of the Christian faith is that, as we accept the compelling invitation to follow Jesus, we are united with innumerable siblings, a family that stretches around the globe and throughout history. Our journey of following and change is a shared adventure; it involves being drawn together into fellowship with people of all kinds.

Hear afresh the call to join the family and to participate in the ultimate adventure: Jesus says, 'Follow me'.

STEVE AISTHORPE

An authority that astonishes

They went to Capernaum, and when the sabbath came, he entered the synagogue and taught. They were astounded at his teaching, for he taught them as one having authority and not as the scribes. Just then there was in their synagogue a man with an unclean spirit, and he cried out, 'What have you to do with us, Jesus of Nazareth? Have you come to destroy us? I know who you are, the Holy One of God.' But Jesus rebuked him, saying, 'Be quiet and come out of him!' And the unclean spirit, convulsing him and crying with a loud voice, came out of him.

Noticing some of the significant elements in today's reading is crucial to understanding many other passages in this gospel. Notice the location: a synagogue. The law stipulated that wherever there were ten Jewish families, there must be a synagogue. Also notice the timing: like so many important incidents in Mark's account, these events took place on the sabbath.

Hearing the teaching of Jesus, the people were astonished and noticed how different it was to what they were accustomed to. It was not that Jesus was exceptional in his eloquence or impressive in his knowledge. Rather, his hearers were astounded by his 'authority'. The norm of the day was for scribes to draw on traditional interpretations they had inherited and learned. They would support their explanations by referring to recognised authorities and quoting from respected sources. However, Jesus spoke with an independent voice.

What happens next continues to demonstrate this unique authority of Jesus. Not only does the gathered congregation recognise it, but so does an 'unclean spirit' (v. 23). The Greek word that Mark uses to describe the bold response of Jesus to the spirit is the same he later applies to Jesus 'rebuking' a storm (Mark 4:39). As we progress through this gospel, we hear and see more and more evidence of Jesus' indisputable sovereignty over sickness, spiritual powers and nature. He says he has authority to forgive sins and, ultimately, demonstrates dominion over death itself.

Take a moment to reflect on the soaring climax of this theme in Jesus' unambiguous declaration: 'All authority in heaven and on earth has been given to me' (Matthew 28:18).

STEVE AISTHORPE

Rhythms of prayer and action

In the morning, while it was still very dark, he got up and went out to a deserted place, and there he prayed. And Simon and his companions hunted for him. When they found him, they said to him, 'Everyone is searching for you.' He answered, 'Let us go on to the neighbouring towns, so that I may proclaim the message there also; for that is what I came out to do.'

Those days in Capernaum were relentless. Jesus was constantly giving out: teaching, healing, setting free the oppressed. The more he did, the more his reputation grew and the demands increased further. We often read of him struggling to find opportunities to be alone in prayer. Rarely were these precious times uninterrupted, and on the occasion we read about today, he needed to rise before dawn to find the solitude he craved.

No doubt Jesus had habits of prayer, but as time went on these were frequently challenged and we see him having to change plans in order to ensure that time with his Father was not squeezed out. In today's passage it is Simon and other companions who manage to find his place of prayer. However, even if they had failed, it would have been only a matter of time before his quiet communion would have been replaced with the pressing demands of crowds, because 'everyone' was searching for him.

We might be tempted to think that Jesus, being the 'Son of God' had no need for the spiritual renewal and guidance that can only be gleaned from prayer. However, as Mark often reminds us, he was also 100% human. Jesus was transparent regarding his total dependence on the Father: 'the Son can do nothing on his own, but only what he sees the Father doing' (John 5:19). The power, compassion and wisdom so evident in all that Jesus said and did flowed from his devotion to his Father. His life was marked by a rhythm of prayerful listening and obedient action. 'I can do nothing on my own', he said (John 5:30).

By encouraging us to pray 'Our Father', Jesus invites us to join with him in an experience he found to be life-giving and indispensable.
Let us pray.

STEVE AISTHORPE

Outsiders become insiders

Jesus went out again beside the sea; the whole crowd gathered around him, and he taught them. As he was walking along, he saw Levi son of Alphaeus sitting at the tax booth, and he said to him, 'Follow me.' And he got up and followed him. And as he sat at dinner in Levi's house, many tax collectors and sinners were also sitting with Jesus and his disciples, for there were many who followed him.

As opposition from religious leaders increased, the context of Jesus' teaching moved from the synagogue into the open air. Capernaum sat on the shore of the lake and was on the main trade route (the 'way of the sea' mentioned in Isaiah 9:1). For the Romans it was a strategic hub for collecting taxes from merchants travelling the highway and fishermen working the lake.

Tax collectors were viewed as having compromised their souls by working for the occupying forces. They were often considered to be grasping and dishonest and were treated with contempt. Levi would have been despised. So imagine the crowd's excitement as Jesus approached the tax booth. How would Jesus confront this greedy traitor?

Yet Jesus' encounter with Levi surprised, shocked and, for some, caused offence. Instead of delivering a rebuke, Jesus issued an invitation to join his growing band of followers. Rather than condemning, he accepted Levi's hospitality and shared a meal with him and a crowd of his detested friends. This was not a gathering where Jesus collected together religious people and invited Levi to join them. No, this was a meal given by Levi to introduce his business associates to Jesus. It was a gathering of 'many' tax collectors and sinners at which Jesus was the chief guest.

From the caustic criticism of his opponents, who called him 'a glutton and a drunkard, a friend of tax collectors and sinners' (Matthew 11:19), we can assume that Jesus joining this kind of gathering was not a one-off event. This was no moral lapse on his part. Rather it was one example of a pattern of behaviour, a deliberate reaching out to people on the fringes of society, to those deemed as unclean or immoral.

Lord, thank you that you love those who are written off by others.
Help me to do likewise. Amen

STEVE AISTHORPE

The Son of Man is Lord

One Sabbath he was going through the grain fields, and as they made their way his disciples began to pluck heads of grain. The Pharisees said to him, 'Look, why are they doing what is not lawful on the Sabbath?' And he said to them, 'Have you never read what David did when he and his companions were hungry and in need of food?… Then he said to them, 'The Sabbath was made for humankind, and not humankind for the Sabbath, so the Son of Man is lord even of the Sabbath.'

Although they were a minority group, the Pharisees feature prominently in the gospels. They believed that the careful interpretation of the law by their trained scribes could produce detailed rules for everyday living. Later in Mark's gospel, we find Jesus confronting them about their habit of neglecting the heart of the law God had given for their own well-being by nitpicking about the minutiae of detailed codes they had developed themselves (7:1–23).

Keeping the sabbath, the fourth commandment, was central to God's plan for an abundant and balanced life for his people. By abstaining from work on the seventh day, people would rest and reinforce their trust in God for provision. Jesus longed for people to realise that the sabbath was created to enrich their lives, not to be a burden or an excuse for failing to extend loving service.

Collecting heads of grain by hand in a neighbour's field was specifically allowed by the law (Deuteronomy 23:25). However, the scribes had developed a list of 39 kinds of 'work' that were forbidden on the sabbath, and the eagle-eyed Pharisees probably reckoned Jesus' followers had violated the ones related to reaping, threshing, winnowing and sorting. By reminding his critics of the time when David's men ate the sacred bread that was given as an offering to God (1 Samuel 21:1–6), Jesus showed that religious piety should never provide an excuse for not helping those in need. The bread that had been offered to God on the altar became sacred again when it was used to feed famished men fleeing for their lives.

Jesus refused to allow hair-splitting and fault-finding to be barriers to helping a person in need, and so should we.

STEVE AISTHORPE

To be with him and to be sent

Jesus went up on a mountainside and called to him those he wanted, and they came to him. He appointed twelve that they might be with him and that he might send them out to preach and to have authority to drive out demons. These are the twelve he appointed: Simon (to whom he gave the name Peter); James son of Zebedee and his brother John (to them he gave the name Boanerges, which means 'sons of thunder'), Andrew, Philip, Bartholomew, Matthew, Thomas, James son of Alphaeus, Thaddaeus, Simon the Zealot and Judas Iscariot, who betrayed him.

Jesus selected these twelve to be his closest comrades and principal representatives after spending the night in prayer (Luke 6:12). For such a crucial decision he certainly needed wisdom from on high, and sometimes that kind of insight is gloriously different to everyday common sense. Jesus' choice of disciples and ambassadors seems surprising to say the least.

The team Jesus picked was a disparate, ragtag collection of men of different backgrounds and education, potentially riven by political and cultural divisions. Simon the Zealot was a passionate nationalist and a sworn enemy of a turncoat tax collector like Matthew (the name it seems that Jesus gave to Levi, meaning 'gift of God'). No HR professional would put together such a team. But Jesus was not interested in who they had been; he was deeply concerned about who they would become.

The purpose of calling the twelve is twofold: 'that they might be with him and that he might send them out'. They are to be 'disciples', those who will follow closely, learn diligently and be his apprentices. And they are to be 'apostles', 'sent ones', messengers, heralds of good news. Jesus has demonstrated his authority over spirits and now he gives them that same capacity. Jesus himself is a sent one, and now he sends others. The learning curve will be precipitous. There will be mistakes and misunderstandings along the way. Over time, 'being with Jesus' and 'being sent' will form these people into those to whom Jesus can say with confidence: 'As the Father has sent me, I am sending you' (John 20:21).

Lord, help me to be constant in being 'with you' and willing and courageous to be 'sent out'. Amen

STEVE AISTHORPE

The seeds of the kingdom

'Listen! A sower went out to sow. And as he sowed, some seed fell on a path, and the birds came and ate it up. Other seed fell on rocky ground, where it did not have much soil, and it sprang up quickly, since it had no depth of soil. And when the sun rose, it was scorched, and since it had no root, it withered away. Other seed fell among thorns, and the thorns grew up and choked it, and it yielded no grain. Other seed fell into good soil and brought forth grain, growing up and increasing and yielding thirty and sixty and a hundredfold.'

Picture the panorama: Jesus is sitting in a boat at the edge of the lake. The crowds line the shore. Behind them, fields stretch into the distance. What could be more natural for the master teacher than to speak in agricultural analogies? The qualities of different soils were both familiar and important to his hearers. Those listening with rapt attention were well acquainted with the difference a well-tilled soil could make to the health or hunger of their family.

Other parables make explicit comparison with the 'kingdom of God' – 'The kingdom of God is as if…' (Mark 4:26); 'With what can we compare the kingdom of God…' (Mark 4:30) – but not here. Perhaps that is because in this parable, Jesus is describing how the kingdom begins: a seed is sown into our lives. Some seeds are fruitful; others fail to thrive. Be assured that the determining factor is not the seed, but the qualities of the soil.

Excellent soil has an openness that allows the roots to go deep and search out nourishment. In contrast, Jesus drew his hearers' attention to the narrow ribbons of ground separating the cultivated fields. It was hard ground, compressed by passing feet, where a seed had no hope of flourishing. The 'rocky ground' was also familiar. Some fields comprised shallow soil on underlying limestone shelves. Being the first areas to warm up made them ideal for rapid germination, but the tender roots of seedlings would soon meet an impenetrable barrier.

What about us? Does the seed find openness?
Will the first roots find nourishment or be frustrated by unbroken ground?
Are there thorns lurking?

STEVE AISTHORPE

The kingdom of God is like...

He also said, 'The kingdom of God is as if someone would scatter seed on the ground and would sleep and rise night and day, and the seed would sprout and grow, he does not know how. The earth produces of itself, first the stalk, then the head, then the full grain in the head. But when the grain is ripe, at once he goes in with his sickle, because the harvest has come.'

The word 'kingdom' appears 162 times in the New Testament. It is central to the teaching of Jesus. In the sermon on the mount he tells us to 'seek first' the kingdom, to pursue it as our highest priority (Matthew 6:33). Jesus proclaimed the kingdom and demonstrated it through his actions. When he sent out his followers, he instructed them to do the same.

Although Jesus never defined the kingdom, he came close when instructing his disciples to pray, 'May your kingdom come. May your will be done on earth as it is in heaven' (Matthew 6:10). In everyday English, the word 'kingdom' refers to the territory over which a king reigns. In the gospels, it denotes the realm over which the 'king of kings' exercises his authority.

This parable of the growing seed appears only in Mark but works with other parables to explain the dynamics of the kingdom. The word translated 'of itself' is the word from which we get the English word 'automatic'. The only other place we find it in the New Testament is when God rescues Peter from jail and the iron gate opened for him 'of its own accord' (Acts 12:10).

The seed does not grow because of the toil of the farmer; it grows 'automatically' or 'by itself'. The farmer has important roles: preparing healthy soil, scattering seed and harvesting. However, make no mistake, the miracle of growth is not dependent on men and women; it is the wonderful, mysterious, often invisible, work of the Creator. Paul knew this well: 'I planted, Apollos watered, but God gave the growth' (1 Corinthians 3:6).

Thank you, Lord, that the thriving and fruiting of the kingdom does not depend upon me. Help me to be faithful in my part and to trust you for what you alone can do. Amen

STEVE AISTHORPE

Why are you afraid?

A great windstorm arose, and the waves beat into the boat, so that the boat was already being swamped. But he was in the stern, asleep on the cushion, and they woke him up and said to him, 'Teacher, do you not care that we are perishing?' And waking up, he rebuked the wind and said to the sea, 'Be silent! Be still!' Then the wind ceased, and there was a dead calm. He said to them, 'Why are you afraid? Have you still no faith?'

What a contrast: seasoned fishermen fear for their lives, terrified by the ferocity of the elements while Jesus sleeps peacefully. What a question: 'Why are you afraid?' I wonder which frightened them most, the storm threatening to drag them into a watery grave or the realisation that the person to whom they had committed their lives had such utter authority over the powers of nature?

When the great Dutch painter Rembrandt depicted this episode in a painting, *The Storm on the Sea of Galilee*, he chose a huge vertical canvas and depicted Jesus and his followers caught in elemental chaos between the raging sea and the clouds. A glance at his picture shows a variety of responses among the boat's occupants. Some, perhaps the veteran sailors, are fighting for control, wrestling with sails or grappling with the rudder. Some, probably focused on their own survival, are clinging on to the ropes that support the mast. At least one is vomiting over the side. One or two appear totally disengaged, in denial regarding what is unfolding. Others are rousing Jesus, or pleading with, questioning or urging him.

One of the remarkable features of Rembrandt's rendering of this scene is that there are not only Jesus and the twelve disciples in the boat. There is an additional person. The artist painted himself into the scene. Have you ever imagined yourself into gospel accounts of encounters with Jesus? This is the perfect passage to try.

Read the scripture again, slowly. Hear the shrieking wind. Feel the violent heaving of the boat. Where are you? How are you responding? Does the storm speak to you of any situation you or others are facing? Now invite Jesus to speak words of authority and peace.

STEVE AISTHORPE

Go in peace

A large crowd followed him and pressed in on him. Now there was a woman who had been suffering from a flow of blood for twelve years. She had endured much under many physicians and had spent all that she had, and she was no better but rather grew worse. She had heard about Jesus and came up behind him in the crowd and touched his cloak, for she said, 'If I but touch his clothes, I will be made well.'

Jesus had just arrived back from the 'other side of the sea' (Mark 5:1), where he had released a man from the oppression of an 'unclean spirit' and, in doing so, destroyed a herd of pigs. The terrified people there had begged him to leave. Then, arriving back, the first person to beg for his attention was a religious leader, Jairus, whose daughter was on the verge of death. It was on the way to respond to his request that Jesus sensed someone touch him. This was no casual brushing past him in the crowd. Someone touched him with intention and with faith. He sensed that 'power had gone forth from him' (v. 30).

Amid the surging crowd, our attention is drawn to one person. This chronically ill woman, destitute after handing over all she had to ineffective healers, also felt a touch. Twelve years of constant bleeding had not only sapped her strength, she had been living with stigma, scorned. Considered unclean, she had endured years of isolation, being cut off from fellowship and communal worship. Suddenly, she knew that the suffering and shame was gone. A new, hope-filled chapter of life had opened.

If that had been the end of the story it would be breathtaking anyway, but the compassion of Jesus led him to halt his journey to powerful Jairus' house and engage in a personal conversation with this woman. As she fell before him in 'fear and trembling' and 'told him the whole truth', he addressed her warmly, affirming her as 'daughter' and sent her on her way with a wonderful blessing: 'Go in peace, and be healed' (vv. 33–34).

Lord, I come to you with empty hands and an open heart.
May I know your peace and healing. Amen

STEVE AISTHORPE

Familiarity breeds contempt

He left that place and came to his hometown, and his disciples followed him. On the Sabbath he began to teach in the synagogue, and many who heard him were astounded. They said, 'Where did this man get all this? What is this wisdom that has been given to him? What deeds of power are being done by his hands! Is not this the carpenter, the son of Mary and brother of James and Joses and Judas and Simon, and are not his sisters here with us?' And they took offence at him.

It was inevitable that word of Jesus' celebrity status would reach Nazareth after all that had been happening down by the Sea of Galilee, in Capernaum and on the other side of the sea – the healings and the crowds awestruck by his powerful teaching. Equally unsurprising is the confusion, contempt and suspicion which he encountered when he arrived home.

Archaeologists estimate Nazareth had a population of about 400 at this time. Everyone would have known Jesus and his family. For those who flocked to see him in other places there was an element of mystery, an eagerness to put a face to the incredible reputation and rumours that were escalating, spreading and multiplying by the day. In his hometown however, associating these extraordinary episodes with the local lad they had known for three decades was a challenge. Could the reports of such incredible happenings really be the work of someone so familiar?

The phrase translated as 'they took offence' conveys the idea of being tripped up. One contemporary translation puts it like this: 'They tripped over what little they knew about him and fell, sprawling' (Mark 6:3, MSG). Their familiarity with Jesus was a stumbling block for them, an obstacle. It created an atmosphere in which the responses and miracles that had occurred elsewhere were not possible. In other places people were astonished by what they saw and heard, but in Nazareth it was Jesus himself who was 'amazed at their unbelief' (Mark 6:6).

Lord, please show me if there is anything in my heart
that might cause me to trip, and may my knowledge of you
never slip into casual familiarity. Amen

STEVE AISTHORPE

You do it

As he went ashore, he saw a great crowd, and he had compassion for them, because they were like sheep without a shepherd, and he began to teach them many things. When it grew late, his disciples came to him and said, 'This is a deserted place, and the hour is now very late; send them away so that they may go into the surrounding country and villages and buy something for themselves to eat.' But he answered them, 'You give them something to eat.'

In Mark's gospel, alongside the remarkable miracles and compelling teaching, we also see the transformation of Jesus' followers. The disciples not only witness the actions and attitudes of the master, they also become involved. They are not passive spectators; they are apprentices and accomplices.

This encounter with a hungry crowd occurs after the disciples return from a tour of villages. Jesus had sent them out to do the same things they had seen him doing. They returned elated, but exhausted. They needed rest and time away with their teacher, but the crowds had other ideas. As Team Jesus escaped by boat, hordes of people pursued them on foot.

Those first disciples had the opportunity to see how the heart and mindset of Jesus contrasted with their own – and so do we. Having planned a restful retreat, the sight of the determined multitude could have been seen as unwanted attention, a nuisance. However, what stirred in Jesus' heart was compassion. He recognised that the hunger drawing the crowd to this remote spot was not for food, but an intense longing for purpose and hope.

Teaching was all very well, but practical concerns weighed on the minds of the disciples: increasing hunger, their remoteness and the lateness of the hour. Again, the contrast between their instincts and the impulse of their rabbi became obvious. To the disciples the answer was clear: 'Send them away.' Jesus had a different proposal: 'You feed them.' I wonder if his alternative idea seemed terrifying or laughable. As events unfolded, this was not just a compassionate response to physical need, it was also the next step in their apprenticeship.

Is there anything that comes to mind where Jesus might be saying,
'You do it'?

? Carol Havey   STEVE AISTHORPE

Take the strain 3am – 6.am

When he saw that they were straining at the oars against an adverse wind, he came towards them early in the morning, walking on the sea. He intended to pass them by. But when they saw him walking on the sea, they thought it was a ghost and cried out, for they all saw him and were terrified. But immediately he spoke to them and said, 'Take heart, it is I; do not be afraid.'

Imagine the scene: a small group of dedicated but weary souls heaving at the oars, far from shore, straining to make headway against the wind, their boat feeling fragile, dwarfed by the expanse of heaving water. I wonder if this will resonate for some people as an apt metaphor for life in a small, fragile church?

For the disciples, the day had started with great excitement. Clustered around Jesus, they had eagerly reported all that had occurred as they had done as he asked, anointing the sick and sharing the message of the kingdom. It had been just as he said. As they stepped out in faith God had been at work. It had been thrilling, but also exhausting.

Jesus' suggestion of time out, with him, was more than welcome, but instead of that there had been more crowds, more need, more giving out. Finally, realising their extreme fatigue, Jesus had packed them off in the boat, dismissed the crowds and found himself a place to pray.

Now weariness had turned to utter exhaustion. They were struggling to make headway against the wind. Jesus was far away, it seemed. Words in John's account of this incident express both the time of day and the prevailing mood: 'It was now dark' (John 6:17).

Then Jesus came to them and their initial shock and fear turned to joy. He may have passed from their minds, but they had never been beyond his awareness. In their state of intense weariness, their awareness of him may have faded, but their struggles had not eluded his attention. During the day he had provided bread; now, in the darkness, he gave protection and assurance.

Whatever challenges may confront you, allow the words of Jesus to seep into your soul: 'Take heart, it is I; do not be afraid.'

STEVE AISTHORPE

Isaiah 1—11

'The vision concerning Judah and Jerusalem that Isaiah son of Amoz saw during the reigns of Uzziah, Jotham, Ahaz and Hezekiah, kings of Judah' (Isaiah 1:1, NIV). Thus spoke Isaiah of Jerusalem to the kingdom of Judah around 742–701 BC. By this time the northern kingdom of Israel had already fallen to the Assyrians, leaving Judah in a perilous situation with potential enemies on all sides. Moreover, Judah had not only external problems, but also serious internal ones. The people frequently turned away from God, and their kings were a very mixed bunch. This led to a considerable amount of injustice and to the oppression of the poor.

Isaiah was a prophet. The first job of a prophet is forthtelling. That is, he was to speak the word of God into the present situation in Judah. His second job was foretelling, looking into the future. In the book of Isaiah we see many examples of foretelling, but it is not always obvious when the prophecies were fulfilled, and indeed whether they have been yet. So some of the prophecies in this early part of Isaiah speak about what will happen to Judah if they don't mend their ways. We now know, of course, that they didn't repent and were defeated by the Babylonians and taken into exile.

But some of the prophecies look forward to much later times. Famously, several point to a coming Messiah, that Christians have long identified as Jesus. If some of the prophecies point to the first coming of Jesus, others appear to refer to the second coming and to the messianic age that will follow. Finally, some of Isaiah's writings contain truths that are timeless and cannot be tied down to any point in history.

In the first eleven chapters of Isaiah, we see a number of key themes. Clearly, Isaiah is extremely concerned about injustice. These readings are scheduled for the season of Advent, where we look forward to both the birth of Jesus Christ and to his second coming. As authors we have long been interested in environmental issues, and a number of the passages we will look at have relevant insights. So come with us now as together we explore the rich resources in Isaiah 1—11.

MARTIN AND MARGOT HODSON

A rebellious nation

Hear me, you heavens! Listen, earth! For the Lord has spoken: 'I reared children and brought them up, but they have rebelled against me. The ox knows its master, the donkey its owner's manger, but Israel does not know, my people do not understand.' Woe to the sinful nation, a people whose guilt is great, a brood of evildoers, children given to corruption! They have forsaken the Lord; they have spurned the Holy One of Israel and turned their backs on him.

A witness is an important person. If a crime has been committed, a witness can give an account of what they saw, making it more likely that justice is served. All creation has been watching Judah's unfaithfulness, and Isaiah calls on the heavens and the earth to be his witnesses.

Isaiah continues to draw on nature when he compares the people's response to God with the loyalty of animals to their owners. There is something special about having a loyal pet, like a dog or a cat who comes to the door when you get home and curls up against you in the evenings. I once cared for a friend's horse while she was on holiday. I found that she came to know me even in a short time, and I was sad to leave her behind. People in Isaiah's day had close relationships with animals for their everyday lives, as much of their world was powered by animals. Isaiah draws on these relationships to challenge God's people on their relationship with God.

It is impossible to fully appreciate the heartbreak of an adult child who turns against their parent. We are made to be in a relationship with God, but when we rebel against God that relationship is damaged. The first few chapters of Isaiah spell out the consequences for God's people, if they continue to behave badly.

It is easy to read these words from a comfortable distance. What ways are we rebelling against God both personally and as a society? Heaven and earth witness our actions – what would Isaiah say to our generation? How does our society treat the most vulnerable in the world and indeed the earth itself? How can we make a difference?

'Your kingdom come, your will be done, on earth as it is in heaven'
(Matthew 6:10).

MARGOT HODSON

The Second Sunday of Advent 117

God longs to forgive

'Come now, let us settle the matter,' says the Lord. 'Though your sins are like scarlet, they shall be as white as snow; though they are red as crimson, they shall be like wool. If you are willing and obedient, you will eat the good things of the land; but if you resist and rebel, you will be devoured by the sword.' For the mouth of the Lord has spoken.

As a vicar, I have found one of the most impractical items of clergy cloth-ing is the surplice. Snowy white, it seems to have a magnetic attraction for Communion wine and lily pollen, both found in abundance in churches, and the latter is almost impossible to remove. I am sure anyone who owns a white shirt, skirt or trousers knows a similar frustration. One small stain can render it unwearable in company!

Stains were no easier to remove in Isaiah's day, and the promise that something crimson could be once again white was promising indeed. It is interesting how early this appears in the text. We might have expected Isaiah to spell out Judah's sins in greater detail before setting out what they needed to do. But, no, Isaiah wants the people to know of God's abundant forgiveness whenever they turn back to him. God longs to see them return to a relationship with him and then be guided into just relationships with people and the rest of creation. His longing is shown in his very early offer to forgive.

But Isaiah is brutally honest – if the people repent and return to God, wonderful things will follow; if, however, they resist and rebel, their world will eventually be destroyed by violence.

We can sometimes become entangled by our past mistakes as they continue to have an impact on our lives, in practical ways and emotionally. Are we willing to admit where we went wrong and place our lives into the gentle cleansing hands of God? Ultimately God's passionate desire to forgive and restore led him, in Christ, to give everything on the cross to break the power of sin and enable forgiveness to flow. All he asks of us is repentance.

'No child of God sins to that degree as to make himself
incapable of forgiveness' (John Bunyan, 1628–88).

MARGOT HODSON

Swords into ploughshares

Many peoples will come and say, 'Come, let us go up to the mountain of the Lord, to the temple of the God of Jacob. He will teach us his ways, so that we may walk in his paths.' The law will go out from Zion, the word of the Lord from Jerusalem. He will judge between the nations and will settle disputes for many peoples. They will beat their swords into plough-shares and their spears into pruning hooks. Nation will not take up sword against nation, nor will they train for war any more.

A ploughshare is the sharp blade of a plough which cuts into the soil when pulled forward by an animal or tractor. We find it most famously in the phrase 'swords into ploughshares', which has been taken from the Bible and is commonly found in speeches and literature concerning disarmament. Public figures in the USA as diverse as founding father Benjamin Franklin, congressman Ron Paul and President Ronald Reagan all used the concept in various ways. It has also been adopted by many peace movements, incorporated into poems and songs, and had artworks devoted to it.

The context into which Isaiah wrote was anything but peaceful. Power-ful enemies surrounded Judah, and eventually the Babylonians destroyed Jerusalem in 587 BC. Isaiah 2:1–5 is a vision of a future time when God will reign from Jerusalem and people of all nations will stream towards it. There will still be disputes between nations, but these will be settled peacefully, with God as the arbiter. There will no longer be any need for weapons, and hence the prophecy of 'swords into ploughshares' will be fulfilled.

Sadly, in spite of all the peace movements, campaigners, Nobel peace laureates and people of goodwill around the world, the kind of peace that Isaiah prophesied seems as elusive as ever. We have seen an example in the terrible consequences that followed the Russian invasion of Ukraine last year. Maybe we should only expect global peace to come when Jesus returns and ushers in the new messianic age. Until then, pray!

'Don't stop after beating the swords into ploughshares, don't stop!
Go on beating and make musical instruments out of them.
Whoever wants to make war again will have to turn them into
ploughshares first' (Yehuda Amichai, 1924–2000).

MARTIN HODSON

Justice for the poor

The Lord takes his place in court; he rises to judge the people. The Lord enters into judgment against the elders and leaders of his people: 'It is you who have ruined my vineyard; the plunder from the poor is in your houses. What do you mean by crushing my people and grinding the faces of the poor?' declares the Lord, the Lord Almighty.

God is on the side of the poor. Isaiah is not the only prophet who tackles the topic; Amos, Ezekiel and Jeremiah were also determined to see justice for the poor. Jesus began his ministry by reading from the scroll of Isaiah, 'The Spirit of the Lord is on me, because he has anointed me to proclaim good news to the poor' (Luke 4:18). Throughout the history of the church, Christians have been following this teaching. The earliest Christians 'sold property and possessions to give to anyone who had need' (Acts 2:45). The medieval Benedictine and Cistercian monasteries cared for those in need. Remember Mother Teresa (1910–97), and think of all the churches currently running food banks. Care for the poor is a very important Christian calling.

In our passage today Isaiah sees God as the judge. Before him in the court are the elders and leaders of the Jewish people. They were responsible for ruining the vineyard, which often represents Israel or the Jewish people in the Bible (see tomorrow's reflection on Isaiah 5). In today's passage the rich elders and leaders are accused of mistreating the poor. Isaiah would almost certainly not have been popular with the leadership, and would have been accused of meddling in things that were not his concern.

How often do we hear politicians chiding church leaders for mixing religion and politics when they make statements criticising policies that they believe are hurting poor and disadvantaged people? Yes, party politics does not mix well with the Christian faith. There are Christians in all major political parties, and opinions vary about the best ways to tackle poverty. Just as Isaiah spoke 'truth to power' in Jerusalem to the rich who crushed the poor, so should our church leaders speak up today and not fear criticism.

'When people say that religion and politics don't mix, I wonder which Bible it is they are reading' (Archbishop Desmond Tutu, 1931–2021).

MARTIN HODSON

The unfruitful vineyard

I will sing for the one I love a song about his vineyard: my loved one had a vineyard on a fertile hillside. He dug it up and cleared it of stones and planted it with the choicest vines. He built a watchtower in it and cut out a winepress as well. Then he looked for a crop of good grapes, but it yielded only bad fruit.

When we moved into our last vicarage, we were delighted to discover that on the back wall there was a vine, planted by one of Margot's predecessors. In our first summer it produced some nice looking grapes. Then we spotted a blackbird coming out of the vine. He and his friends had eaten all our grapes! The next year we had a much better plan. Our gardener carefully pruned the vine in February, and through the spring we saw a bumper crop of grapes developing. This time we went to the garden centre and got a huge roll of netting which we cunningly draped from the upstairs windows to protect our grapes from the birds. In October we harvested the grapes, and took them round to a member of our congregation, who specialised in making wine. Around Christmas time he presented us with four bottles of Chateau Hodson! It really was very good, and for the following years we repeated the whole process, and the wine got better and better.

On a rather larger scale, the owner of the vineyard in our reading today also did everything possible to get a good harvest. But unlike our grapevine, the grapes were all bad. Who was represented in the vineyard, and why were the grapes bad? In Isaiah 5:7 we find out: 'The vineyard of the Lord Almighty is the nation of Israel, and the people of Judah are the vines he delighted in. And he looked for justice, but saw bloodshed; for righteousness, but heard cries of distress.' God gave Judah all they needed, but as we have seen already in these reflections, the people and their leaders frequently turned away.

There are nearly 200 mentions of vines and vineyards in the Bible, and often they are used as illustrations and allegories. Can you think of some?

'I am the true vine, and my Father is the gardener' (John 15:1).

MARTIN HODSON

Social injustice

Woe to you who add house to house and join field to field till no space is left and you live alone in the land. The Lord Almighty has declared in my hearing: 'Surely the great houses will become desolate, the fine mansions left without occupants. A ten-acre vineyard will produce only a bath of wine; a homer of seed will yield only an ephah of grain.'

We live in a village where a philanthropist has had a lasting influence. Sir Stafford Cripps lived in Filkins, Oxfordshire in the middle of the last century. He built a village centre, a shop, a swimming pool and a bowling green as well as financing low-cost housing. His positive influence can still be felt in the good facilities and housing that local people can afford to rent. Isaiah prophesied against a very different kind of people. Society was changing from one where wealth was widely spread, to one where there were a few rich people and many who were barely managing. Those with power and wealth were taking everything for their own profit, squeezing out the poor and the powerless. His message is stern – they will find themselves alone in the land, which will fail to produce its harvests.

What do we see in our own society? In many parts of the UK, people find it hard to rent a home because so many houses and flats have been converted into holiday lets. Many are only just managing with incomes that barely cover the cost of living. If we look globally, countries in the global north are vastly better off than those in the global south, and we have unprecedented numbers of refugees and migrants. What would Isaiah say to our nation, and how can we respond to his prophecy?

We are in the season of Advent. This is a time when we are called to examine our lives and see what needs to be reset. What can we do? How about donating some Christmas grocery items to the local food bank? Do you have friends or relatives who would be pleased to receive a charity gift card, indicating help given overseas, rather than a present?

'What can I give him, poor as I am?… Yet what I can I give him: give my heart' (Christina Rossetti, 1830–94).

MARGOT HODSON

Isaiah's vision in the temple

In the year that King Uzziah died, I saw the Lord, high and exalted, seated on a throne; and the train of his robe filled the temple. Above him were seraphim, each with six wings: with two wings they covered their faces, with two they covered their feet, and with two they were flying. And they were calling to one another: 'Holy, holy, holy is the Lord Almighty; the whole earth is full of his glory.'

If you enter the chancel of our village church in Filkins, you will find the roof is painted deep blue, is covered with stars and has the words 'Holy, Holy, Holy' written across a high beam. It is as if the heavens are in the church and, by entering the church, you have entered into the presence of God, just as Isaiah did all those centuries ago.

Isaiah's exceptional vision was life changing. He had always been faithful to God and had long been concerned by the injustice and apostasy of his people, but his vision of God crystallised his faith and confirmed his calling. If we read on, we find that when faced with God in all his glory, he was totally ashamed, aware of his unworthiness (vv. 4–8). I wonder what words he remembered to make him aware of his unclean lips, or was it simply that he was so conscious of the wrongs of his own people that he fully identified with them himself? As a future messenger, he needed cleansed lips, and after that symbolic cleansing, comes the call from God: 'Whom shall I send? And who will go for us?' Isaiah does not hesitate, 'Here am I. Send me!' (v. 8).

In Hebrew the phrase 'Here I am' is just one word *Hineni*. It is the response that Moses gave to the voice from the burning bush, and Samuel used the same word when God called him in the temple. It reveals an eagerness and complete willingness to respond to God's calling. Let us make this Advent a time when we respond *Hineni* to God, always remembering that God has also said *Hineni* to us.

'Here I am! I stand at the door and knock. If anyone hears my voice and opens the door, I will come in and eat with them, and they with me' (Revelation 3:20).

MARGOT HODSON

123

Isaiah's difficult calling

'Go and tell this people: "Be ever hearing, but never understanding; be ever seeing, but never perceiving." Make the heart of this people calloused; make their ears dull and close their eyes. Otherwise they might see with their eyes, hear with their ears, understand with their hearts, and turn and be healed.'

I have been to many ordination services where Isaiah 6 has been read, ending in a crescendo of 'Here am I. Send me!' The new ministers are sent out with an optimistic vision – God is with them and will surely bless their work for him. But the passage always ends at verse 8, and the harsh reality of Isaiah's call (vv. 9–10) is not mentioned. For however faithful we are to our churches, careers, families and other responsibilities, success does not always follow and it is easy to feel we have failed. How do we understand God's call, when we have been faithful and yet things have not thrived?

Isaiah had an incredible vision of God; he responded to God's call but then the crunch came. Far from having a 'successful' ministry with lots of people responding to his message, God warns Isaiah that his message will be ignored. This chapter starts unusually with a king's death, and Isaiah's calling is placed after society's ills have been mapped out in earlier chapters. Isaiah saw that the nation would inevitably fall. However, the scale of corruption meant that the people could not see their lifestyles clearly.

This echoes our severe contemporary predicament. Scientists have been calling us to respond to the seriousness of the environmental crisis for years, yet so often we respond with dull ears, cloudy eyes and unreached hearts. We see it and yet we pull back from letting the reality sink in. We do not believe that our culture could also fail as the climate spins out of control. Like Isaiah, let us speak truth, examine our own lives and be faithful to all that God calls us to.

---

*'O God of the poor, help us to rescue the abandoned and forgotten
of this earth, so precious in your eyes. Bring healing to our lives,
that we may protect the world and not prey on it,
that we may sow beauty, not pollution and destruction'
(Pope Francis).*

MARGOT HODSON

The 'with us God'

Again the Lord spoke to Ahaz, 'Ask the Lord your God for a sign, whether in the deepest depths or in the highest heights.' But Ahaz said, 'I will not ask; I will not put the Lord to the test.' Then Isaiah said, 'Hear now, you house of David! Is it not enough to try the patience of humans? Will you try the patience of my God also? Therefore the Lord himself will give you a sign: the virgin will conceive and give birth to a son, and will call him Immanuel.'

Many years ago, I had a fellowship at the Hebrew University in Jerusalem, researching plant science. It was suggested that I learn a little Hebrew, and although I am not a great linguist I took up the challenge. I never became fluent, but I could understand quite a bit that was spoken and read it fairly well.

I became a Christian that year in Jerusalem. I attended Christ Church, just inside Jaffa Gate in the Old City. In the chancel there is a large Communion table with a Hebrew inscription along the top of the front, 'Do this in remembrance of me.' In the centre of the front, a prominent black disc with gold symbols and writing has a crown at the top and a Star of David below it. Sandwiched between the two is 'Immanuel' in Hebrew script. This symbolises that Immanuel is king of Israel. *Im* means 'with'. *Immanu* is 'with us.' So *Immanuel* is 'with us God'. I always liked that. It was in Jerusalem that I came to realise that the 'with us God' was with me. He has never left me.

Now well into the season of Advent we look forward to celebrating Jesus' birth. Immanuel only appears two more times in the whole Bible: once shortly after our reading, in Isaiah 8:8, and then in Matthew 1:23. Matthew cites Isaiah, stating that the birth of Jesus the Messiah was the fulfilment of his prophecy. This was some 700 years after Isaiah's time. The 'with us God' came to be with us in human form, the incarnation, just as Isaiah had predicted. May God be with us as we ponder the miracle of the incarnation this season.

Emmanuel: God with us! God is so close to us!

MARTIN HODSON

Holiness of God

The Lord Almighty is the one you are to regard as holy, he is the one you are to fear, he is the one you are to dread. He will be a holy place; for both Israel and Judah he will be a stone that causes people to stumble and a rock that makes them fall. And for the people of Jerusalem he will be a trap and a snare.

We can reflect on three words in this passage: holy, fear and stone.

First, *holy*. The context of this passage is that King Ahaz has ignored Isaiah's advice and made an alliance with Assyria. Ahaz was not a good king and not infrequently worshipped other gods and made sacrifices to them on high places, including one of his sons. Holy is a word that is difficult to define, but includes the concepts of saintliness, devotion, piety and being set apart. Ahaz was none of these. But the Lord Almighty will be set apart as holy.

Second, *fear*. 'I am going to put the fear of God into him!' This sort of threat is perhaps especially associated with a teacher in a school many years ago glowering at a particularly naughty pupil. But we also use the phrase 'God-fearing' to describe a person of firm faith and convictions. What does 'the fear of God' actually mean? It certainly includes awe and reverence for God, and not just the shaking-in-our-boots sort of fear. But it definitely includes that sort of fear, and that is intended in our passage: 'He is the one you are to dread' (v. 13).

Third, *stone*. Both the northern kingdom, Israel, and the southern kingdom, Judah, are seen to stumble over the stone, a holy place, that represents the Lord Almighty. First Israel and then Judah turned away from the Lord, and went after other gods and unholy alliances. It is not popular nowadays to see God as a judge. A loving, kind God is fine, but a God of judgement is not. But if we look in the Bible it is quite clear that both facets of divinity are included. Our God is a just judge, but he *is* a judge.

'Know that the Lord has set apart his faithful servant for himself;
the Lord hears when I call to him' (Psalm 4:3).

MARTIN HODSON

Light in a dark land

Nevertheless, there will be no more gloom for those who were in distress. In the past he humbled the land of Zebulun and the land of Naphtali, but in the future he will honour Galilee of the nations, by the Way of the Sea, beyond the Jordan. The people walking in darkness have seen a great light; on those living in the land of deep darkness a light has dawned.

Isaiah's never-perceiving people were heading into trouble. Their leaders' poor judgement was causing disintegration of the nation, which would ultimately fall. What hope was there in this dark situation? God may judge his people, but he never leaves them without the promise of restoration, and here this is described as light in a dark land.

Light and darkness is a significant Advent theme. The time of judgement gives us a space to examine our lives and rethink our ways of living. We do this knowing that God longs to bring us out of darkness and into light.

This century has not been an easy one so far, with wars, a pandemic, recession and the climate crisis. As we examine our lives during Advent, we can also look at our wider society, realising that climate change is a crisis of our own making and the pandemic is likely to have come from our damaging approach to nature. Like Isaiah's never-perceiving people, many fail to make the connections that might lead to positive change. Do we as Christians have a role in this? Environmentalist Gus Speth said: 'I used to think that the top global environmental problems were biodiversity loss, ecosystem collapse and climate change… but I was wrong. The top environmental problems are selfishness, greed and apathy, and to deal with these we need a spiritual and cultural transformation. And we lawyers and scientists don't know how to do that.'

As followers of Christ let us pray for guidance for how we can be bearers of light for those living in dark times. The birth of Christ affirms God's love for the whole creation and his coming light is a promise of restoration and an opportunity for us to see our lives afresh. In looking for light, we need it most in our hearts. Only then can we share light with others.

'Come you indoors, come home; your fading fire. Mend first and vital candle in close heart's vault' (Gerard Manley Hopkins, 1844–89).

MARGOT HODSON

A child is born

For to us a child is born, to us a son is given, and the government will be on his shoulders. And he will be called Wonderful Counsellor, Mighty God, Everlasting Father, Prince of Peace. Of the greatness of his government and peace there will be no end. He will reign on David's throne and over his kingdom, establishing and upholding it with justice and righteousness from that time on and forever. The zeal of the Lord Almighty will accomplish this.

Meanings of names are often an important consideration when parents are naming their newborn, and they were especially significant in ancient cultures. In biblical times, Pharaohs and other rulers were given special names when they came to power, denoting expectations for their reign. The titles in today's passage fit within these formal names of the ancient world and the original hearers would have seen them as a promise of a king in their time who would lead their nation out of its difficulties and be a wise leader, strong protector and caring father to their people and who would secure lasting peace.

Isaiah's words echo down the generations and, from earliest times, Christians have seen this promise as a prophecy of the birth of Jesus. Human rulers will always have their limitations, but the birth of Jesus signalled something new. Fully human and yet mighty God, one small child is born to be the Saviour of the world.

With Christmas almost upon us, it is good to reflect on these titles and the amazing gift that Jesus is to each one of us. The ancient Egyptians might have hoped for these qualities in fear that the new Pharaoh would be far from any of them. We can look to the coming of Jesus with knowledge that he has all these qualities and more. One day he will return to reign – until then let him rule our hearts and lives.

Many carols have been inspired by this text, and you might like to look out for them as they are sung in Christmas services.

'Hail the heaven-born Prince of Peace! Hail the Sun of Righteousness!
Light and life to all he brings, risen with healing in his wings'
(Charles Wesley, 1707–88).

MARGOT HODSON

The peaceable kingdom

A shoot will come up from the stump of Jesse; from his roots a Branch will bear fruit. The Spirit of the Lord will rest on him – the Spirit of wisdom and of understanding, the Spirit of counsel and of might, the Spirit of the knowledge and fear of the Lord.

As we approach the end of our reflections on the first eleven chapters of Isaiah, we come to one of the most well-known passages in the whole book. Isaiah 11:1–11 was the inspiration for a famous series of paintings produced around the 1830s by Edward Hicks. *The Peaceable Kingdom* depicted a future harmony between wild and domesticated animals and between animals and humanity (see tomorrow's reflection for more on this).

The phrase 'peaceable kingdom' comes from the King James Bible of 1611, which headed chapter 11 with 'The peaceable kingdome of the Branch out of the root of Jesse'. This heading is not part of the original Hebrew text, and is not used in more modern translations, but the phrase stuck. It became a theological concept, and Stanley Hauerwas used the phrase as the title of his renowned book on Christian ethics. The idea has gone well beyond theology – there are books, songs, films and games based on it, many of which are in the secular realm.

The peaceable kingdom sounds amazing, but how do we get to this future harmonious state? Our passage today is another of Isaiah's messianic prophecies: 'A shoot will come up from the stump of Jesse'. Jesse was the father of King David, and this indicates that the Messiah will come from the line of Jesse and David. Christians have long held that the Messiah prophesied in this passage is Jesus. Certainly, the characteristics given here to the Messiah sound a lot like Jesus. The Spirit of the Lord gives him wisdom, understanding, counsel, might, knowledge and fear of the Lord. It is only when Jesus the Messiah returns that we can expect to see the peaceable kingdom fully brought in.

'The narratives of Scripture were not meant to describe our world…
but to change the world, including the one in which we now live'
(Stanley Hauerwas).

MARTIN HODSON

The wolf and the lamb

The wolf will live with the lamb, the leopard will lie down with the goat, the calf and the lion and the yearling together; and a little child will lead them. The cow will feed with the bear, their young will lie down together, and the lion will eat straw like the ox. The infant will play near the cobra's den, and the young child will put its hand into the viper's nest. They will neither harm nor destroy on all my holy mountain.

Have you ever wondered what the new creation will be like? Here in Isaiah 11 we get some clues. But what strange clues! The wolf and the lamb, the leopard and the goat, and the calf and the lion. Will lions really eat straw? Will all animals, including humans, be vegetarian or vegan? What can all this mean? As a biologist it definitely seems an odd world. Inevitably there are many people who see this passage as figurative, so not to be taken literally. New Testament scholar Richard Bauckham takes this view, and says that a vegetarian lion would be so different as to be another species. I agree with him!

Here in Isaiah 11 is a picture of future harmony, and of peace (*shalom*). We see harmony between wild and domesticated animals, and between animals and humanity, represented by a little child. The new creation will be a peaceable kingdom where animals and humanity are reconciled. Clearly, biological processes will be very different from those we see today. We are not at all sure how this will be brought about, or what it will look like. But this new harmony will involve all creatures and not just humans. We will no longer live in an anthropocentric world. It is the kind of harmony that we should be working towards.

However, we don't have to wait for the new creation to help bring in a little of it. There is a lot we can do at an individual, community, national or even international level. Maybe you could form a group within your church to look into what can be done, or maybe you can join one that already exists. The environmental crisis is extremely serious and we all need to be involved in helping to solve it.

'The new creation surpasses Eden, but one could also say that it realises the potential of Eden' (Richard Bauckham).

MARTIN HODSON

Also by **Martin and Margot Hodson**…

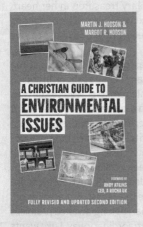

**A Christian Guide to
Environmental Issues**

9781800390058
£9.99

Green Reflections
Biblical inspiration for sustainable living

9781800390683
£8.99

To order, visit **brfonline.org.uk** or use the form on page 151.

Living Faith

Christmas

'Just what I really wanted!' We all enjoy surprises at Christmas, especially those thoughtful, imaginative gifts which show that we are known and valued.

Even more so for that first Christmas, which Luke narrates for us in some detail. His careful research gives us the fullest description we have of those events which Mary treasured in her heart, reflecting on them over the years. Over this next week we will be pondering with her. We aim to share her amazement in seeing how God chose to give that gift for which our hearts long.

However, the problem for us is that this astonishing story is just too familiar. Countless nativity plays have dulled any sense of shock in seeing how God enters our world in the babe of Bethlehem. We need to see how much more wonderful is that first nativity than the one we may hold in our minds, often conceived when we ourselves were young children.

For Luke gives special treatment to his nativity story, which he concludes with Jesus' genealogy from Adam. He deliberately uses a particular writing style similar to the Septuagint (that is, the Greek version of the Old Testament) to show the continuity of the gospel of Jesus with the Hebrew scriptures. He is picking up, so to speak, from where the Jewish Bible leaves off.

For God is patiently at work over the millennia. His long-awaited promises to the people of Israel are to be fulfilled in an extraordinary way. Luke wants us to know God is true to his covenant. He wants us to have the fullest confidence in his word so that we may receive this breathtaking gift ourselves.

Furthermore (and this comes as a real surprise) it does not matter who we are or even where we are. God can use anyone, anywhere, as the nativity narrative demonstrates. So we need to be alert to his purposes and his prompting. Prepare to be surprised!

Over this next week ask the Holy Spirit to help you enter that first Christmas with delight and wonder, to appreciate that this is news of great joy for all peoples everywhere. Above all, we seek to behold the baby wrapped in swaddling clothes and laid in a feeding trough, for you and us all.

ROSS MOUGHTIN

Daring to trust

The angel answered, 'The Holy Spirit will come on you, and the power of the Most High will overshadow you. So the holy one to be born will be called the Son of God. Even Elizabeth your relative is going to have a child in her old age, and she who was said to be unable to conceive is in her sixth month. For no word from God will ever fail.' 'I am the Lord's servant,' Mary answered. 'May your word to me be fulfilled.' Then the angel left her.

This is it! The longings of the years, even over the millennia, are about to be met, and to be met in a way that no one anticipated. God is coming to redeem his people, all people, and remarkably he looks for the assent of a young woman living in Nazareth in Galilee.

Nazareth! Nowhere is Nazareth mentioned in the Hebrew scriptures; it is just an ordinary, everyday town. While Mary herself is no one special: she is young and a woman, and probably, as we will see, from a poor family. Not even married, simply betrothed to a craftsman. Yet the angel Gabriel suddenly appears to her with a startling message: God has chosen her to give birth to a son, even 'the Son of the Most High' to reign from David's throne forever.

But this is how God prefers to work, through those of low status – the disadvantaged and disregarded. For what God is looking for is a simple willingness to trust him, to do his will even in the most taxing of circumstances: obedience rather than ability is the key.

At first Mary is thrown off balance by the encounter, trying to make sense of what is happening. But soon she regains her composure and simply asks how God is going to do this. Effectively, the angel responds: 'Through you.' No doubt God has been preparing Mary for this moment, gently affirming step-by-step simple decisions of trust, unremarkable in themselves but teaching her to trust in his faithfulness. For God is asking a lot; she knows her reputation and that of Joseph is going to be besmirched. Who is going to believe her? And yet she believes in God's promise and so she says 'Yes'.

And that yes, freely given, is going to change the world.

Lord, in big and small ways teach me to trust you.

ROSS MOUGHTIN

A channel for God's amazing gift

'My soul glorifies the Lord and my spirit rejoices in God my Saviour, for he has been mindful of the humble state of his servant. From now on all generations will call me blessed, for the Mighty One has done great things for me – holy is his name… He has filled the hungry with good things but has sent the rich away empty. He has helped his servant Israel, remembering to be merciful to Abraham and his descendants forever, just as he promised our ancestors.'

No doubt Mary's mind was racing as she hurried some distance south to meet with her relative Elizabeth. Clearly she needed to share her extraordinary experience with someone she could trust, to make sense of the angel's amazing message.

And no sooner had she arrived when the baby in Elizabeth's womb leaps for joy at the sound of Mary's greeting. For Mary this is a vivid vindication of her decision to trust God's word. No wonder her heart is filled with joy as it all comes together in her thinking. Truly God is at work, and at work even through her.

Then she gives voice to this joy in a canticle of praise, glorifying God for his unique blessing. She rejoices that he has chosen her, a lowly servant girl, to deliver his blessings to a troubled and weary world. Truly God is a God of unchanging grace, steadfast over the generations! Her profound understanding of the Hebrew scriptures gives context to her encounter with the angel Gabriel. So she claims for herself the song of Hannah made generations earlier (1 Samuel 2:1–10). Like Mary, Hannah was also blessed by God in a remarkable way through the gift of a child, the prophet Samuel. This is the God who turns our social order on its head, who roots for the downtrodden and prioritises the poor.

Moreover, Mary understands that she is part of God's fundamental purpose of blessing all families of the earth beginning with the call of Abraham. His faithful obedience to step out into the unknown stands as an example to Mary. On this special day may we too allow God to bless others through us.

'Where meek souls will receive him, still the dear Christ enters in'
(Phillips Brooks, 1835–93). Amen.

ROSS MOUGHTIN

As good as done!

'Praise be to the Lord, the God of Israel, because he has come to his people and redeemed them. He has raised up a horn of salvation for us in the house of his servant David (as he said through his holy prophets of long ago), salvation from our enemies and from the hand of all who hate us – to show mercy to our ancestors and to remember his holy covenant, the oath he swore to our father Abraham to rescue us from the hand of our enemies, and to enable us to serve him without fear in holiness and righteousness before him all our days.'

Zechariah praises God at the ceremony which he and his wife thought would never happen, the circumcision of their own son. It must have been a deeply moving experience for these elderly parents, only too aware of God's special favour when they had all but given up on having children.

And no sooner is John named than his father regains the ability to speak, and straightaway he honours God in a paean of praise. But these are no ordinary words, they are from God himself, a prophecy inspired by the Holy Spirit. We still use them today in church.

What makes his canticle so extraordinary is that Zechariah praises God not simply for the gift of his own son but for the gift of another child, a son of the house of David. He describes this promised child as being 'a horn of salvation', an image used in the Hebrew scriptures to convey God's incredible strength, even the assurance of his victory over all that would overwhelm us.

This long-awaited visitation of God is about to happen as he fulfils his promise to Zechariah's forefather Abraham to bless his people so that they may share his holiness and righteousness. Whether he realises this or not, Zechariah is speaking of Jesus, even though Jesus is yet to be born, and in keeping with the tradition of the Hebrew prophets, he uses the past tense to describe an event in the future. For such is God's faithfulness that when he promises to act, it is as good as done.

May we have Zechariah's confidence in God's word.

ROSS MOUGHTIN

Where God finds no room

In those days Caesar Augustus issued a decree that a census should be taken of the entire Roman world. (This was the first census that took place while Quirinius was governor of Syria.) And everyone went to their own town to register… While they were there, the time came for the baby to be born, and she gave birth to her firstborn, a son. She wrapped him in cloths and placed him in a manger, because there was no guest room available for them.

Jesus is born, not in Nazareth, where Mary and Joseph were to live, but in Bethlehem, the town of King David. Joseph had little choice but to obey the imperial decree and register in his ancestral home some 70 miles away. Presumably he chose to take Mary with him on what was not an easy journey for an expectant mother.

Clearly Caesar Augustus would appear to be in charge here, but the reality is that God himself is using this edict from Rome for his particular purpose. Not that anyone would have realised this at the time. Wonderfully, God is committed to the prophecy he gave to Micah centuries earlier, that the Messiah would be born in Bethlehem.

Intriguingly we do not know whether Mary and Joseph, as they made the long journey, were aware of the significance of their destination. Even so, Luke in his account gives no sense of rush and no mention of innkeepers, nor in fact of any inn as some modern translations bear witness. Rather, the key phrase is 'no guest room'. Wherever Mary and Joseph were staying, there was no room for the newborn Jesus. Sadly people have been denying him room ever since.

What of the manger? This is a significant detail for Luke: he mentions it three times: It was probably made from or hewn from stone and separated the home's living quarters from where the animals would sleep overnight.

Who would have thought, as Mary has little choice but to place her firstborn into this feeding trough, that 'the hopes and fears of all the years are met in thee tonight'? This is how God enters his world, how he sets his glory aside.

Where do we deny Jesus room?

ROSS MOUGHTIN

A startling sign

And there were shepherds living out in the fields near by, keeping watch over their flocks at night. An angel of the Lord appeared to them, and the glory of the Lord shone around them, and they were terrified. But the angel said to them, 'Do not be afraid. I bring you good news that will cause great joy for all the people. Today in the town of David a Saviour has been born to you; he is the Messiah, the Lord. This will be a sign to you: you will find a baby wrapped in cloths and lying in a manger.'

No one trusted shepherds, and people kept their distance from them to avoid being made ritually unclean and therefore excluded from worshipping with God's people. They were the classic outsiders, the underclass. They may even have been, like David centuries earlier, older children. Even so these shepherds proved faithful to the care of their sheep, living in the fields to keep their flock safe throughout the night.

God sends his angels, his messengers, with extraordinary news of great joy. The longings over the centuries are this night decisively answered, even within running distance! At last the Messiah is born: a Saviour for shepherds, and so for everyone. No wonder the shepherds are completely overwhelmed with the sight and sounds of that night.

The angel sends them to welcome the newborn Jesus and to encourage Mary and Joseph, with the praises of the heavenly host still ringing in their ears.

Once again Luke mentions the manger, clearly not what these shepherds would have expected for such a special baby. The swaddling bands, wrapped tightly around the newborn baby, are also significant, literally. For they point to how the body of the crucified Jesus will be wrapped in a linen cloth, confined in a stone-hewn tomb – until they are cast aside in the resurrection.

This truly is a time for celebration! As the heavenly host praise the glory of God and his purpose to transform this troubled earth with his grace, only these shepherds are privileged to hear their song. For everyone else in Bethlehem, just a normal night, nothing special.

Lord, may I see what you are showing me.

ROSS MOUGHTIN

A gift for everyone

Now there was a man in Jerusalem called Simeon, who was righteous and devout. He was waiting for the consolation of Israel, and the Holy Spirit was on him… When the parents brought in the child Jesus to do for him what the custom of the Law required, Simeon took him in his arms and praised God, saying: 'Sovereign Lord, as you have promised, you may now dismiss your servant in peace. For my eyes have seen your salvation, which you have prepared in the sight of all nations: a light for revelation to the Gentiles, and the glory of your people Israel.'

Now an old man carefully takes the baby Jesus in his arms and blesses him. His waiting is over. As ever, God proves faithful to his promise to comfort his people. Mary and Joseph travel just five miles to the temple at Jerusalem to consecrate their firstborn to the Lord. For this devout Jewish couple, the temple was at the very heart of their faith, the place where God dwells with his people.

What they could not have realised is that their decision enabled God to keep his promise to Simeon 'that he would not die before he had seen the Lord's Messiah' (v. 26). This is the moment as the Holy Spirit draws Simeon into the temple court at precisely the right time and shows him that this is the baby, this is the long-awaited Messiah.

How he knows, Luke does not explain. There would seem nothing special about Mary and Joseph, who could only afford the minimum sacrifice allowed in the law of the Lord, just a pair of doves or two young pigeons rather than the usual lamb.

Such is Simeon's joy that he instinctively praises God for allowing him this special moment. Surely this is God at work in a way which exceeds his expectations, for this holy child is given not simply for the salvation of the people of Israel. Amazingly he is a gift for everyone, even as a light to the Gentiles.

This is it! Not just for the people of Israel but for the whole human family. Hallelujah!

Praise God for his faithfulness!

ROSS MOUGHTIN

An astonishing boy

After three days they found him in the temple courts, sitting among the teachers, listening to them and asking them questions. Everyone who heard him was amazed at his understanding and his answers. When his parents saw him, they were astonished. His mother said to him, 'Son, why have you treated us like this? Your father and I have been anxiously searching for you.' 'Why were you searching for me?' he asked. 'Didn't you know I had to be in my Father's house?' But they did not understand what he was saying to them.

Fast-forward twelve years. Mary and Joseph are back at the temple in Jerusalem for the annual Passover festival. Now Jesus is no longer a dependent child but on the cusp of manhood, a member of the covenant people of God in his own right. Joseph and Mary travel home to Nazareth in their respective groups before realising at the end of their first day's walk that Jesus is not with them, and so they return to fetch him. You can sense both their relief and frustration in Mary's rebuke when to their evident surprise they finally find him in the temple.

Jesus responds by saying that this is the most obvious place for him to be and describes the temple as his Father's house. For this is his priority. Already Jesus knows that he has a special status in God, knowing the Lord God of Israel, the creator of heaven and earth, even as Father. This distinct understanding was to be at the very heart of his ministry, of his very identity.

But this astonishing self-awareness is clothed in humility as Jesus sits among the teachers listening to them and asking them questions. He is still learning, still growing but by all accounts his answers show a remarkable maturity.

Moreover, as Luke makes clear, he is to return to Nazareth where he continues to honour Mary and Joseph through his obedience. Joseph's role is in no way supplanted by Jesus' insight. And that is it for another 18 years or so, before Jesus begins his breathtaking ministry.

Father, thank you that in finding Jesus
I know that I am your precious child.

ROSS MOUGHTIN

Great expectations

The people were waiting expectantly and were all wondering in their hearts if John might possibly be the Messiah. John answered them all, 'I baptise you with water. But one who is more powerful than I will come, the straps of whose sandals I am not worthy to untie. He will baptise you with the Holy Spirit and fire. His winnowing fork is in his hand to clear his threshing-floor and to gather the wheat into his barn, but he will burn up the chaff with unquenchable fire.'

We are getting very close now, and people sense that God's Messiah is about to appear. They long to be freed from Caesar with his legions and the whole imperial apparatus. They resent being subject to Gentiles with their pagan gods.

John the Baptist would seem to be an obvious candidate. His tough and uncompromising message of a radical new start with God is certainly pulling in the crowds. They were even prepared to be baptised rather than simply rely on their birth to become a member of God's covenant people. But the man himself is quite clear. He is not the Messiah, but the voice of one preparing for his coming, merely fulfilling Isaiah's ancient prophecy of getting his people ready for the arrival of God's kingdom.

Nevertheless, John explains that the coming of the Christ is close at hand and that his ministry would be so much more powerful than his. John baptised with water simply as a sign of God's blessings to come. The Messiah would baptise, yes, but his baptism would be, so to speak, the real thing. He would baptise with the Holy Spirit of God himself. This baptism would be by fire as well as water, purifying as well as cleansing, as spoken of by the Hebrew prophets. It would be so much more thorough and life-changing than John's baptism, of a different order altogether.

God is about to reap his harvest, to bring together his own. But even John, as he was soon to discover, was not able to fully comprehend the extent of God's wonderful grace to be realised in his relative, Jesus of Nazareth.

Lord, may I expect great things of you. Amen

ROSS MOUGHTIN

SHARING OUR VISION – MAKING A GIFT

I would like to make a donation to support BRF.
Please use my gift for:

☐ Where the need is greatest   ☐ Anna Chaplaincy   ☐ Living Faith
☐ Messy Church   ☐ Parenting for Faith

Title	First name/initials	Surname
Address		
		Postcode
Email		
Telephone		
Signature		Date

Our ministry is only possible because of the generous support of individuals, churches, trusts and gifts in wills.

Please treat as Gift Aid donations all qualifying   *giftaid it*
gifts of money made (*tick all that apply*)

☐ today,   ☐ in the past four years,   ☐ and in the future.

I am a UK taxpayer and understand that if I pay less Income Tax and/or Capital Gains Tax in the current tax year than the amount of Gift Aid claimed on all my donations, it is my responsibility to pay any difference.

☐ My donation does not qualify for Gift Aid.

Please notify BRF if you want to cancel this Gift Aid declaration, change your name or home address, or no longer pay sufficient tax on your income and/or capital gains.

You can also give online at **brf.org.uk/donate**, which reduces our administration costs, making your donation go further.

Please complete the other side of this form ➔

SHARING OUR VISION – MAKING A GIFT

Please accept my gift of:

☐ £2 ☐ £5 ☐ £10 ☐ £20 Other £ [   ]

by (*delete as appropriate*):

☐ Cheque/Charity Voucher payable to 'BRF'

☐ MasterCard/Visa/Debit card/Charity card

Name on card

Card no. [ ][ ][ ][ ] [ ][ ][ ][ ] [ ][ ][ ][ ] [ ][ ][ ][ ]

Expires end [M][M] [Y][Y] Security code* [ ][ ][ ] *Last 3 digits on the reverse of the card

Signature | Date

☐ I would like to leave a gift to BRF in my will.
Please send me further information.

☐ I would like to find out about giving a regular gift to BRF.

For help or advice regarding making a gift, please contact our fundraising team +44 (0)1235 462305

Your privacy

We will use your personal data to process this transaction. From time to time we may send you information about the work of BRF that we think may be of interest to you. Our privacy policy is available at **brf.org.uk/privacy**. Please contact us if you wish to discuss your mailing preferences.

Registered with

FUNDRAISING **REGULATOR**

↪ Please complete the other side of this form

Please return this form to 'Freepost BRF'
No other address information or stamp is needed

Bible Reading Fellowship is a charity (233280) and company limited by guarantee (301324), registered in England and Wales

ND0323

Overleaf… Reading *New Daylight* in a group | Author profile |
Recommended reading | Order and subscription forms

Reading New Daylight in a group

GORDON GILES

It is good to talk. While the Rule of Benedict, which formed the spiritual foundations of the daily prayer life of so many ecclesiastical foundations, recommended daily scripture reading as a key aspect of the community life of work and prayer, discussion and reflection are a good consequence of reading passages that others are reading simultaneously. Separated by space, as each reads alone, we are yet connected by the common food of scripture, taken in our own time and at our own pace. We each chew on it in our own way. Yet discussion or shared reflection on the passages chosen and the comments made can aid digestion, so here are some open questions that may enable discussion in a Bible study or other group who gather to take further what is published here. The same questions may also aid personal devotion. Use them as you wish, and may God bless and inspire you on your journey as you read, mark and inwardly digest holy words to ponder and nourish the soul.

General discussion starters

These can be used for any study series within this issue. Remember there are no right or wrong answers – these questions are simply to enable a group to engage in conversation.

- What do you think is the main idea or theme of the author in this series? Did that come across strongly?

- Have any of the issues discussed touched on personal – or shared – aspects of your life?

- What evidence or stories do the authors draw on to illuminate, or be illuminated by, the passages of scripture.

- Which do you prefer: scripture informing daily modern life, or modern life shining a new light on scripture?

- Does the author 'call you to action' in a realistic and achievable way? Do you think their ideas will work in the secular world?

- Have any specific passages struck you personally? If so, how and why? Is God speaking to you through scripture and reflection?

- Was anything completely new to you? Any 'eureka' or jaw-dropping moments? If so, what difference will that make?

Questions for specific series

Autumn (Sheila Walker)

- Might there be such a thing as a 'spiritual autumn' in our lives? In what ways might this be either an encouragement or a cause for concern?
- Looking back, what colours predominate in your life? How might the passing of time lend a different perspective?
- How might we encourage one another to 'bear fruit in every season'?
- Do you have unfulfilled dreams, maybe God-given ones? How might you explore or pursue them further?
- How are your spiritual roots? How might God be wanting to refresh them?
- Choose a simple, everyday object, such as a piece of fruit, a glove, a knife, a pencil or a cup. Spend five to ten minutes in silence, just looking and wondering at it, then share your thoughts.

Bible meals (Ruth Hassell)

- When have you known God's invitation to come, sit and eat?
- What is it about eating together that deepens friendships and relationships?
- What is it that stops us from inviting others in?
- How do we celebrate in times of uncertainty without it feeling forced and out of step?
- Who are the people in your community who are not yet around the table of your church?
- Where are the unexplored opportunities in your community to offer hospitality?

Romans (Bob Mayo)

- God's calling on Paul's life was not for a special honour, but for a special responsibility; he was to be the apostle for the Gentiles. What are the particular people, tasks or concerns that you feel God has given you a responsibility for?

- How do you understand salvation, past, present and future, in your life?

- The idea that God reveals himself through the creation brings a particular urgency to the debate about how to care for the environment. Are there excuses for not being aware of the issues at hand?

- Church is not an optional extra. Christianity is a shared faith; church is where our belief comes to life, and we collectively live out our righteousness through faith. What are the strengths (and weaknesses) of the church of which you are a part?

- By drawing on the example of Abraham's faith, Paul is looking back to see forward; he is drawing on the stories of the past to learn lessons for the future. Who have been the heroes of the faith for you and what are the lessons they have taught you?

- Suffering can be transformative. Two people can meet the same situation; it can drive one of them to despair, and in another it can create a sense of hope. Do you have stories of suffering through which you or others have grown as a person?

Isaiah 1—11 (Martin and Margot Hodson)

- What were the key problems that beset the kingdom of Judah at the time when Isaiah wrote chapters 1—11?

- Outline the main roles of a prophet. Where do we see these exercised in chapters 1—11?

- Is it realistic to hope that 'swords into ploughshares' might happen in the present age?

- Isaiah is incredibly concerned about injustice. What can we learn from him that is relevant to us today?

- The Hodsons are passionate about the environment and creation care. How do they link this concern to the passages they considered in Isaiah 1—11? How much is this linkage justified?

- What do you think the new creation will look like? Does it bear any resemblance to Isaiah's vision in chapter 11?

- Have you been able to link these readings from Isaiah 1—11 to your own Advent journey this year? How has Isaiah spoken to you?

Meet the author: Roland Riem

How did you come to faith?

At the age of 17 I was close friends with two other boys at school. One became a Christian and then the other. My turn came soon after, when the curate at my friends' church came to the school to speak, explaining how Jesus had died for me and how I could let him into my heart. I did so at the bus stop immediately afterwards and found the aforesaid heart duly warmed! Since then my journey has been through almost all the traditions of the Church of England and learning from many others, especially Benedictine.

What have you done in faith and ministry up till now?

I've been in cathedral ministry for almost as long as I can remember, which I like because of the many creative ways in which one can engage with the world as a place of history, culture and spirituality. Teaching has always been a part of my ministry. I like the challenge of making big ideas accessible and giving people ways into the breadth, height and depth of God's love. For example, it can be fun to offer the genealogy at the start of Matthew's gospel to a large group of vergers to help them to find their own place in history.

Who has inspired you and why/how?

When my mother died she left a letter explaining a little of our family history, which she had been secretive about. It set me on a trail exploring my Jewish origins on her side. (Her parents were Russian, originally from Ukraine, though she was born in Berlin.) The last decade or so I have been learning to see the gospel more inclusively and sympathetically for those who cannot accept Jesus in established Christian terms. I am also blessed to be married to an artist whose work enables me to see faith expressed in beauty and colour.

What are your hobbies and interests?

One major interest as the years go by is finding ways to prevent my body from seizing up. My wife and I are walking the South West Peninsular and we are currently halfway round. We pack a wide selection of braces for ankles and knees and look forward to arriving at each B&B for a hearty supper. I have also been playing tennis for over 50 years and in all that time have mastered just one stroke, the lob, which can be annoying for both the opposition and me.

Recommended reading

The message of the kingdom of God: an ecology of equality and peace, and an economy of justice. Hope from beyond, sent to the present, is what Advent asks us to reckon with. Hope consists of God's jump leads sent from the future through time and space, wired right into our present pains, panics and predicaments. How can the light of Christ illuminate this present darkness?

An Advent Manifesto engages with two great Christmas hymns: the Magnificat and Benedictus. It is also rooted in poets, prophets and the theology and devotional writing of Howard Thurman, the black theologian and mentor to Martin Luther King Jr. Using the *lectio divina* approach to passages drawn from Isaiah and Luke, this book is an invitation to pray and practise that most ancient Advent prayer: 'Come, Lord Jesus, come.'

The following is an edited extract taken from the introduction.

This book was conceived at a time of enormous global turmoil. Government buildings in Washington DC had been stormed by supporters of Donald Trump. Black Lives Matter ferments with regular eruptions of protest. The world was gripped by a global pandemic that was seeing millions die. The European Union was squabbling over vaccines. Europe is at war for the first time in 70 years, with the very survival of Ukraine under threat. There are grain and gas shortages, which is driving up the cost of living. 'Food security' is now an issue, with a war pushing the price of fuel, food and fertiliser so high that nations are starving.

As though that was not enough to contend with, the politics of liberal democracies seem to be failing. Populism and extremism are becoming mainstream. Campaigns for equal rights – ethnicity, disability, sexuality and gender – are experiencing unprecedented pushback and encountering renewed hostility and oppression. In a world of turmoil and turbulence, there seems to be a decline in reason and responsibility, and ever-increasing privileging of unaccountable power and passionate intensity.

In the midst of this, refugees and asylum seekers are symptoms of wars, famines and political rights being denied in countries that were once progressive. Meanwhile, the church is beset with internal wrangling on sexuality, gender, declining numbers and collapses in revenue. There is a serious growing crisis of mental health among clergy, and a marked fragmentation in ecclesial systems of governance, with the institution experienced as increasingly irrelevant in the public sphere.

It is against this background that I thought I might try to write a book about the second coming of Christ. It is an Advent book, but also a reminder to me as much as it might be to any reader, that the life, work, focus, deeds and words of Jesus are about ushering in the kingdom of God, not propping up the church. Put another way, seek first the kingdom of God and God's righteousness and some of these other things may be added to you (Matthew 6:33). Matthew's beatitudes continue with a caveat for us to heed: 'For each day has enough worries of its own.' Quite so. We are called to abide in the uncertainty and trouble of life. There is no other life to live with.

Sometimes the church can seem to seek almost every available prop and lever of support it can, leaving the kingdom of God largely to itself and certainly forgetting about the righteousness of God. So we should not lose sight of our sin (it is within us, so not always easy to spot and call out, though others will see it). Our Advent must be framed in the context of the inexhaustible mercy and redemption of God.

God's love has consequences. As love arrived in the person of Jesus, unbidden and unmerited, so our love for others – especially 'the least' – must be unbidden too. Any love given is only ever unmerited, in the same way that none of us can earn or deserve God's love. So, we love because God first loved us (1 John 4). We didn't start this chain reaction. God is the originator. Love has come; it has arrived in Jesus. What will you return to God for this free, undeserved, infinite and inexhaustible gift?

This book is very much about the politics of paradise and consequences of God's love for us all. It takes as its cue one of the fundamental cores of liberation theology and many other kinds of liberation theologies, that all good religion worthy of the name of religion and faith is inherently political. If politics is about who gets what, when, where and how, the kingdom of God, if nothing else, is about precisely the same. The poor, the lame, the hungry, the marginalised and the stigmatised all receive God's kingdom first.

To order a copy of this book, please use the order form on page 151 or visit **brfonline.org.uk**

Enjoy a little luxury: upgrade to *New Daylight deluxe*

Many readers enjoy the compact format of the regular *New Daylight* but more and more people are discovering the advantages of the larger format, premium edition, *New Daylight deluxe.* The pocket-sized version is perfect if you're reading on the move but the larger print, white paper and extra space to write your own notes and comments all make the deluxe edition an attractive alternative and significant upgrade.

Why not try it to see if you like it? You can order single copies at brfonline.org.uk/newdaylightdeluxe

Deluxe actual size:

gladness instead of mourning, the mantle of spirit. They will be called oaks of righteousness to display his glory.

We learn from these verses that gladness is first them' gladness instead of mourning and praise in gift needs to be received, and action is often re gift. For example, receiving a piano is of little us play it. God has blessed us with 'every spiritual but, metaphorically speaking, *we* have to pour o put on and wear the mantle of praise. The Lord

To order

Online: **brfonline.org.uk**
Telephone: +44 (0)1865 319700
Mon–Fri 9.30–17.00

Delivery times within the UK are
normally 15 working days. Prices are
correct at the time of going to press
but may change without prior notice.

Title	Price	Qty	Total
Christmas Voices	£9.99		
The Living Cross	£8.99		
Celebrating Christmas	£9.99		
A Christian Guide to Environmental Issues	£9.99		
Green Reflections	£8.99		
An Advent Manifesto (BRF Advent book)	£9.99		
Working from a Place of Rest (new edition)	£9.99		

POSTAGE AND PACKING CHARGES			
Order value	UK	Europe	Rest of world
Under £7.00	£2.00		
£7.00–£29.99	£3.00	Available on request	Available on request
£30.00 and over	FREE		

Total value of books	
Postage and packing	
Donation*	
Total for this order	

* Please complete and return the
Gift Aid declaration on page 141.

Please complete in BLOCK CAPITALS

Title _____ First name/initials _____ Surname_____

Address_____

_____ Postcode _____

Acc. No. _____ Telephone _____

Email_____

Method of payment

☐ Cheque (made payable to BRF) ☐ MasterCard / Visa

Card no. ⬚⬚⬚⬚ ⬚⬚⬚⬚ ⬚⬚⬚⬚ ⬚⬚⬚⬚ ⬚⬚⬚⬚ ⬚⬚⬚

Expires end ⬚M⬚M ⬚Y⬚Y   Security code ⬚⬚⬚   Last 3 digits on the reverse
of the card

We will use your personal data to process this order. From time to time we may send you information
about the work of BRF. Please contact us if you wish to discuss your mailing preferences **brf.org.uk/privacy**

Please return this form to:
BRF, 15 The Chambers, Vineyard, Abingdon OX14 3FE | enquiries@brf.org.uk
For terms and cancellation information, please visit brfonline.org.uk/terms.

BRF needs you!

If you're one of our many thousands of regular New Daylight readers you will know all about the rich rewards of regular Bible reading and the value of daily notes to guide, inform and inspire you.

Here are some recent comments from *New Daylight* readers:

'Thank you for all the many inspiring writings that help so much when things are tough.'

'Just right for me – I learned a lot!'

'We looked forward to each day's message as we pondered each passage and comment.'

If you have similarly positive things to say about *New Daylight*, would you be willing to help spread the word about these popular resources? Could you follow the example of long-standing *New Daylight* reader Beryl Fudge and form a *New Daylight* reading group, not to take the place of private prayer and reading but to share insights and deepen understanding. 'I've quite a few friends who also take the notes and we discuss them in the group,' says Beryl. 'There's so much in them every day. What I most value in *New Daylight* is the way that they connect the Old and New Testament scriptures with what's happening here and now.'

It doesn't need to be complicated: every issue of *New Daylight* includes questions for reflection or discussion.

We can supply further information if you need it and would love to hear about it if you do form a *New Daylight* reading group.

For more information:

- Email **enquiries@brf.org.uk**
- Telephone BRF on +44 (0)1865 319700 Mon–Fri 9.30–17.00
- Write to us at BRF, 15 The Chambers, Vineyard, Abingdon OX14 3FE

Enabling all ages to grow in faith

At BRF, we long for people of all ages to grow in faith and understanding of the Bible. That's what all our work as a charity is about.

- Our **Living Faith** range of resources helps Christians go deeper in their understanding of scripture, in prayer and in their walk with God. Our conferences and events bring people together to share this journey, while our Holy Habits resources help whole congregations grow together as disciples of Jesus, living out and sharing their faith.

- We also want to make it easier for local churches to engage effectively in ministry and mission – by helping them bring new families into a growing relationship with God through **Messy Church** or by supporting churches as they nurture the spiritual life of older people through **Anna Chaplaincy**.

- Our **Parenting for Faith** team coaches parents and others to raise God-connected children and teens, and enables churches to fully support them.

Do you share our vision?

Though a significant proportion of BRF's funding is generated through our charitable activities, we are dependent on the generous support of individuals, churches and charitable trusts.

If you share our vision, would you help us to enable even more people of all ages to grow in faith? Your prayers and financial support are vital for the work that we do. You could:

- support BRF's ministry with a regular donation
- support us with a one-off gift
- consider leaving a gift to BRF in your will
- encourage your church to support BRF as part of your church's giving to home mission – perhaps focusing on a specific ministry or project
- most important of all, support BRF with your prayers.

Donate at **brf.org.uk/donate** or use the form on pages 141–42.

Endings and beginnings

Therefore, if anyone is in Christ, the new creation has come: the old has gone, the new is here!

2 CORINTHIANS 5:17 (NIV)

This last quarter of the year is an interesting intersection of endings and beginnings. For many, September marks the start of a new school year, with all the challenges and opportunities that may bring. At the same time, we begin to see the end of the calendar year in sight. These beginnings and endings can be a useful time to reflect on the time past and the time to come.

For BRF's ministries, this time is a mixture of reflection and preparation. **Anna Chaplains** across the country are bringing fellowship and spiritual care to older people during this period where loneliness can be exacerbated. The **Living Faith** team are busy preparing resources to help people to explore their faith in the important seasons of Advent and, looking ahead, Lent. For **Messy Church**, this can be a busy quarter of the year, with many Messy Churches restarting after a summer break and planning ahead for the busy Christmas period. And our **Parenting for Faith** team are working to support parents and churches as many things change for children during this period.

While our work is constantly changing, we embrace the message of the Bible verse above – the old has gone, the new is here. We are excited for all the new ideas and projects we will be exploring in the months to come and we celebrate all that we have already accomplished in 2023.

Our vital work would not be possible without kind donations from individuals, charitable trusts and gifts in wills. If you would like to support BRF's work now and in the future you can become a Friend of BRF by making a monthly gift of £2 a month or more – we thank you for your friendship.

Find out more at **brf.org.uk/donate** or get in touch with us on **01235 462305** or via **giving@brf.org.uk**.

Judith Moore
Fundraising development officer

Give. Pray. Get involved.
brf.org.uk

NEW DAYLIGHT SUBSCRIPTION RATES

Please note our new subscription rates, current until 30 April 2024:

Individual subscriptions
covering 3 issues for under 5 copies, payable in advance
(including postage & packing):

	UK	Europe	Rest of world
New Daylight	£19.05	£26.55	£30.45
New Daylight 3-year subscription (9 issues) (not available for Deluxe)	£54.45	N/A	N/A
New Daylight Deluxe per set of 3 issues p.a.	£24.15	£33.00	£39.00

Group subscriptions
covering 3 issues for 5 copies or more, sent to one UK address (post free):

New Daylight	£14.85 per set of 3 issues p.a.
New Daylight Deluxe	£18.75 per set of 3 issues p.a.

Please note that the annual billing period for group subscriptions runs from 1 May to 30 April.

Overseas group subscription rates
Available on request. Please email **enquiries@brf.org.uk**.

Copies may also be obtained from Christian bookshops:

New Daylight	£4.95 per copy
New Daylight Deluxe	£6.25 per copy

All our Bible reading notes can be ordered online by visiting **brfonline.org.uk/subscriptions**

New Daylight is also available as an app for Android, iPhone and iPad
brfonline.org.uk/apps

NEW DAYLIGHT INDIVIDUAL SUBSCRIPTION FORM

All our Bible reading notes can be ordered online by visiting
brfonline.org.uk/subscriptions

Title _____ First name/initials _____ Surname _____

Address _____

_____ Postcode _____

Telephone _____ Email _____

Please send *New Daylight* beginning with the January 2024 / May 2024 /
September 2024 issue (*delete as appropriate*):

(*please tick box*)	UK	Europe	Rest of world
New Daylight 1-year subscription	☐ £19.05	☐ £26.55	☐ £30.45
New Daylight 3-year subscription	☐ £54.45	N/A	N/A
New Daylight Deluxe	☐ £24.15	☐ £33.00	☐ £39.00

Optional donation* to support the work of BRF £ _____

Total enclosed £ _____ (cheques should be made payable to 'BRF')

*Please complete and return the Gift Aid declaration on page 141 to make your
donation even more valuable to us.

Please charge my MasterCard / Visa with £ _____

Card no. ☐☐☐☐ ☐☐☐☐ ☐☐☐☐ ☐☐☐☐

Expires end ☐☐ ☐☐ Security code ☐☐☐ Last 3 digits on the reverse of the card

To set up a Direct Debit, please complete the Direct Debit instruction on page 159.

We will use your personal data to process this order. From time to time we may send you
information about the work of BRF. Please contact us if you wish to discuss your mailing
preferences **brf.org.uk/privacy**

Please return this form with the appropriate payment to:
BRF, 15 The Chambers, Vineyard, Abingdon OX14 3FE
For terms and cancellation information, please visit **brfonline.org.uk/terms**.

Bible Reading Fellowship is a charity (233280) and company limited by guarantee (301324),
registered in England and Wales

ND0323

☐ I would like to give a gift subscription (please provide both names and addresses):

Title _____ First name/initials _____ Surname _____

Address _____

_____ Postcode _____

Telephone _____ Email _____

Gift subscription name _____

Gift subscription address _____

_____ Postcode _____

Gift message (20 words max. or include your own gift card):

_____

_____

Please send *New Daylight* beginning with the January 2024 / May 2024 / September 2024 issue (*delete as appropriate*):

(*please tick box*)	UK	Europe	Rest of world
New Daylight 1-year subscription	☐ £19.05	☐ £26.55	☐ £30.45
New Daylight 3-year subscription	☐ £54.45	N/A	N/A
New Daylight Deluxe	☐ £24.15	☐ £33.00	☐ £39.00

Optional donation* to support the work of BRF £ _____

Total enclosed £ _____ (cheques should be made payable to 'BRF')

*Please complete and return the Gift Aid declaration on page 141 to make your donation even more valuable to us.

Please charge my MasterCard / Visa with £ _____

Card no. ☐☐☐☐ ☐☐☐☐ ☐☐☐☐ ☐☐☐☐

Expires end ☐☐ ☐☐ Security code ☐☐☐ Last 3 digits on the reverse of the card

To set up a Direct Debit, please complete the Direct Debit instruction on page 159.

We will use your personal data to process this order. From time to time we may send you information about the work of BRF. Please contact us if you wish to discuss your mailing preferences **brf.org.uk/privacy**

Please return this form with the appropriate payment to:
BRF, 15 The Chambers, Vineyard, Abingdon OX14 3FE
For terms and cancellation information, please visit **brfonline.org.uk/terms**.

Bible Reading Fellowship is a charity (233280) and company limited by guarantee (301324), registered in England and Wales

You can pay for your annual subscription to our Bible reading notes using Direct Debit. You need only give your bank details once, and the payment is made automatically every year until you cancel it. If you would like to pay by Direct Debit, please use the form opposite, entering your BRF account number under 'Reference number'.

You are fully covered by the Direct Debit Guarantee:

The Direct Debit Guarantee

- This Guarantee is offered by all banks and building societies that accept instructions to pay Direct Debits.

- If there are any changes to the amount, date or frequency of your Direct Debit, Bible Reading Fellowship will notify you 10 working days in advance of your account being debited or as otherwise agreed. If you request Bible Reading Fellowship to collect a payment, confirmation of the amount and date will be given to you at the time of the request.

- If an error is made in the payment of your Direct Debit, by Bible Reading Fellowship or your bank or building society, you are entitled to a full and immediate refund of the amount paid from your bank or building society.

- If you receive a refund you are not entitled to, you must pay it back when Bible Reading Fellowship asks you to.

- You can cancel a Direct Debit at any time by simply contacting your bank or building society. Written confirmation may be required. Please also notify us.

Instruction to your bank or building society to pay by Direct Debit

Please fill in the whole form using a ballpoint pen and return with order form to:
BRF, 15 The Chambers, Vineyard, Abingdon OX14 3FE

Service User Number: | 5 | 5 | 8 | 2 | 2 | 9 |

Name and full postal address of your bank or building society

To: The Manager	Bank/Building Society
Address	
	Postcode

Name(s) of account holder(s)

Branch sort code

☐☐ – ☐☐ – ☐☐

Bank/Building Society account number

☐☐☐☐☐☐☐☐

Reference number

☐☐☐☐☐☐

Instruction to your Bank/Building Society

Please pay Bible Reading Fellowship Direct Debits from the account detailed in this instruction, subject to the safeguards assured by the Direct Debit Guarantee. I understand that this instruction may remain with Bible Reading Fellowship and, if so, details will be passed electronically to my bank/building society.

Signature(s)

Banks and Building Societies may not accept Direct Debit instructions for some types of account.

Enabling all ages to grow in faith

Anna Chaplaincy

Living Faith

Messy Church

Parenting for Faith

BRF is a Christian charity that resources individuals and churches. Our vision is to enable people of all ages to grow in faith and understanding of the Bible and to see more people equipped to exercise their gifts in leadership and ministry.

To find out more about our work, visit

brf.org.uk